Towards the Single Employment Contract

This book examines the concept of the single employment contract, tracing it from its genesis and evaluating its pros and cons in the context of the current labour market problems in selected European countries.

The book adopts a comparative approach to examining the single employment contract, highlighting its virtues and revealing its inherent contradictions. The authors set out the general framework within which the current debate has developed by outlining the origins that gave rise to the proposal of a single employment contract. They then review the debate on labour market segmentation and the flexicurity proposal, and examine the key characteristics of the single employment contract as well as the arguments put forward both for and against it. Case studies show how the idea has been taken up in France, Italy and Spain. The book concludes with a concise review of contractual arrangements in EU labour markets and of possible future projections and developments.

The book is aimed at academics and practitioners interested in labour market and labour legislation reforms.

Towards the Single Employment Contract

Comparative Reflections

GIUSEPPE CASALE AND ADALBERTO PERULLI

·HART·
PUBLISHING

HART PUBLISHING • OXFORD AND PORTLAND, OREGON
INTERNATIONAL LABOUR OFFICE • GENEVA
2014

Published in the United Kingdom by Hart Publishing Ltd
16C Worcester Place, Oxford, OX1 2JW
Telephone: +44 (0)1865 517530
Fax: +44 (0)1865 510710
E-mail: mail@hartpub.co.uk
Website: http://www.hartpub.co.uk

Published in North America (US and Canada) by
Hart Publishing
c/o International Specialized Book Services
920 NE 58th Avenue, Suite 300
Portland, OR 97213-3786
USA
Tel: +1 503 287 3093 or toll-free: (1) 800 944 6190
Fax: +1 503 280 8832
E-mail: orders@isbs.com
Website: http://www.isbs.com

Published in Switzerland by the
International Labour Office
4, Route des Morillons
CH-1211 Geneva 22
Telephone: +41 22 799-7370
Fax: +41 22 799-6938
E-mail: pubvente@ilo.org
Website: http://www.ilo.org/publications

British Library Cataloguing in Publication Data

Data Available

ISBN: 978-1-84946-581-6 (Hart)

ISBN 978-92-2-127491-9 (ILO)

Typeset by Hope Services Ltd, Abingdon
Printed and bound in Great Britain by
TJ International Ltd, Padstow, Cornwall

Foreword

Here is a timely work. It arrives just at the right moment. The expression *contrat de travail unique* (*single employment contract*) is no longer reserved in its usage to a circle of insiders originating from academic backgrounds. From now on it is part of the language used by national and international administrations. It therefore deserves to be subject to an extensive enquiry so that the context in which it appeared and the sense given to it may be explained.

The success of the expression does not mean that there is agreement as to what it represents. That is the foremost virtue of this book. It shows meticulously, rigorously and with equanimity what makes up the intellectual construct which today is called, not without qualification, the single employment contract. This book is, therefore, as timely as it is well conceived. The exercise was, however, a difficult one, notably because this concept is becoming established in proposals intended to guide actions – in reform projects, in other words. The concept therefore owes much to the diagnosis which justifies these proposals and, striking closer still to the origins of the issue, to the ways in which this diagnosis is made.

The authors know everything about this genesis. Hence they reveal the roots of projects which highlight the promotion of the single employment contract. If incorporated into reforming speeches, the concept could have no more unity than the various programmes which refer to it. However, this book endeavours to bring unity into focus, before summarizing the various forms the concept assumes in some countries whose governments are seduced by or interested in the virtues of reform undertaken under the banner of the single employment contract.

Rigorous in researching origins and presuppositions, precise in its presentation of experiences, this book does not conceal anything of the debate to which the single employment contract gives rise. Is it hopeful or illusory? Enthusiasms, doubts and criticisms are reported in a balanced way.

After reading this book, each individual will thus be more confident in his or her analysis and proposals.

Antoine Lyon-Caen

Acknowledgements

We would like to take this opportunity to thank the colleagues, students and friends who contributed in one way or another to the preparation of this volume.

We are particularly grateful to ILO colleagues Mario Fasani and Humberto Villasmil who contributed with critical suggestions.

Special appreciation goes to Charlotte Beauchamp, Chris Edgar and Alison Irvine of ILO Publishing for all their support and personal commitment to this project.

Many thanks to all of them.

g.c.
a.p.

Contents

Table of Legislation

National

France

Italy

Spain

European Union

International

Introduction

The New Frontier of Labour Law: Between Freedom and Security

In open societies, labour law and its protection model, built around the employment contract, represent one of the major forms of 'governmentality'.[1] Operating within a framework antithetical to that of the pure market (represented by the deployment of capital according to purely economic and commercial logic), and characterized by the interaction of collective actors, labour law has, for more than a century, protected individuals within market economies from social and economic insecurity. Today, this model is in crisis, under pressure from economic globalization and the concomitant trends towards labour flexibility and the disintegration of the traditional employment relationship. Together, these phenomena have reintroduced high levels of risk and uncertainty into the labour environment. The dynamics of labour demand and supply have become part of a mercantile calculation of manufacturing and functional requirements, subordinated to the imperative of maximizing value creation for players in an economy that, in the view of many, has been reduced to the condition of a casino.[2]

According to the most critical analyses, this neo-mercantile approach to labour is reducing the individual to the status of an 'economic resource'. The current terminology of human capital, employability and flexibility reflects a view of individuals not as human beings, but as things that share characteristics with materials – a view that corresponds, in the world of law, to the dissolution of established legal categories into a cybernetic school of management thinking.[3]

Within legal systems, this recommodification of labour, and the progressive loss of the social security that was guaranteed by the Fordist compromise, is leading to a rethinking of labour market regulation and the emergence of new guarantees and security features. The dialectic between freedom and security, typical of the history of capitalism, needs to find a new balance, with new forms of security sufficiently

[1] On the notion of governmentality, see Foucault, M, *Sécurité, Territoire, Population: Cours au Collège de France (1977–1978)* (Paris, Seuil/Gallimard, 2004).

[2] This is the view of, among others, Supiot, A, *L'esprit de Philadelphie* (Paris, Seuil, 2009) 137.

[3] Ibid, 143.

versatile to structure labour markets adequately in a diverse and changing context. Efforts are under way to construct new arrangements capable of compensating for the loss of the social rights that were built around the standard employment contract, pre-eminently the loss of employment stability.

In the new labour market, which has become simply a locus of commodity exchange, where professional trajectories are interrupted and fragmented, protection is increasingly offered by new devices of welfare, more or less reliable and generous, under the rubric of 'flexicurity'. On closer examination, the 'flexicurity' model is based on a view of work as 'goods', the loss of which can be compensated for by a subsidy or allowance. It seems that work is treated as a sort of 'toxic asset', from which the enterprise can be freed through the intervention of the state.[4] This simplistic view, based on the monetization of the economic value of work, takes no account of the non-monetary value of work that ultimately gives substance to the social and personal development of the worker.

As the structure of the labour market undergoes continuous and complex change, owing to various combinations of market and social responses that are not always easy to analyse and interpret, so the position of the worker in the market is also gradually changing. In an ever more globalized economy, characterized by unprecedented competition not only between enterprises, but between legal systems[5] and social systems,[6] we are also witnessing a competition among workers, played out on the world stage, with unrelenting downward adjustment of working and living conditions. Everything seems to turn on the 'capacity' of the provider of labour to be comparatively more attractive in the human resources market.

Today, the dualism and segmentation of the labour market separates not just insiders and outsiders, but also, and increasingly, insiders from other insiders – the only differentiating factor being whether or not the worker has the guarantee of an employment contract. The existence of significant segments of the labour market crowded with low-skilled, temporary and intermittent workers raises concerns about the ability of labour law in its current form to play its traditional role as a social integrator and as an antidote to the commodification of work. Updating the classic analysis of the 'dual' labour market[7] to take contemporary conditions into account reveals a dramatic aggravation of that original dualism, characterized by the multiplication of categories of workers within a general rise of uncertainty or *montée des incertitudes*.[8] Temporary contracts and labour flexibility can be a real 'trap' which undermines the possibility of long-term employment,[9] obscuring – if not abolishing – the virtues

---

4 See Del Conte, M, 'L'influenza del diritto comunitario sul diritto del lavoro italiano fra tutele e flessibilità' in *Studi in Onore di Tiziano Treu* vol III (Napoli, Jovene, 2011) 1448.

5 See Deakin, S, 'Legal Diversity and Regulatory Competition: Which Model for Europe?' (2006) 12(4) *European Law Journal* 440 ff.

6 See Rigaux, M, *Droit du travail ou droit de la concurrence sociale?* (Bruxelles, Bruylant, 2011).

7 See Doeringer, P and Piore, M, *Internal Labour Markets and Manpower Analysis* (Lexington, Heath Books, 1971).

8 See Castel, R, *La montée des incertitudes: Travail, Protection, Statut de l'individus* (Paris, Seuil, 2009).

9 See Eyraud, F and Vaughan-Whitehead, D, 'Employment and Working Conditions in the Enlarged EU: Innovations and New Risks in F Eyraud and D Vaughan-Whitehead (eds), *The Evolving World of Work in the Enlarged EU. Progress and Vulnerability* (Geneva, ILO, 2007) 26 ff.

associated with work and the identity with work. The historical polarization between the human as a labouring animal and the creative worker *homo faber*[10] seems to be recurring in the post-industrial labour market, with its high proportions of technological artisans, temporary workers and permanent outsiders.

Other important phenomena arising in the post-Fordist economy are contributing to the changed appearance of the labour market. With the advent of cognitive capitalism, the connection between work and knowledge is being strengthened by a new legislative trend towards the de-standardization and individualization of work within a framework of administration that is increasingly discretionary and differentiated at enterprise level.[11] The ambiguity inherent in the neo-individualist dimension of so-called 'knowledge work' is reflected in both the nature of the work and the new 'protagonism' of the worker. On the one hand, the work is now conceived not as (mere) 'work' but as 'action' that contributes to the process of building a 'common world'; on the other hand, the very meaning of the relationship between work and the individual is called into question by the de-socialization and self-exploitation triggered by the competitive individualism that characterizes the new global labour market.

The changes currently transforming markets and enterprises are not affecting paid work alone, but extend into the areas of autonomous work and the various forms of 'economic dependence'. For these segments of the labour market too, the core issue is that of security. The task at hand here is not simply to absorb the economic dependence of the self-employed person into the realm of subordinate employment, but to understand how proposed new ways of structuring work and its regulation relate to work across the whole spectrum from autonomy to subordination.[12]

The new balance between freedom and security, then, should cover the future of labour relations in the long term, offsetting the high social risks associated with the increasing casualization of work and ensuring that 'atypical', temporary work does not mean a lifetime of insecurity but can constitute the first step in a long-term career. New active labour market policies, therefore, must create and maintain institutional bridges that foster professional growth for all workers. One way of achieving this objective is by streamlining the multitude of types of employment contract, especially in systems with highly segmented labour markets, and enhancing the flexibility of the standard employment contract of unlimited duration (in respect of internal, numerical and functional flexibility, education and training).

This is where the idea of the single employment contract comes in, offering a reduction in the multiplicity of different types of employment contract, strongly associated with precarious work, and their consolidation into a single container contract, in return for greater flexibility for enterprises in dismissing workers, with concomitant protection for workers through 'flexicurity' measures. It was suggested by the European Commission's Green Paper on modernizing labour law in 2006, and

[10] See Arendt, H, *The Human Condition* (Chicago, University of Chicago Press, 1958).

[11] See Moulier Boutang, Y, *Le capitalisme cognitif* (Paris, Editions Amsterdam, 2007).

[12] See the analysis of Freedland, M, 'From the Contract of Employment to the Personal Work Nexus' (2006) 35(1) *Industrial Law Journal* 1 ff.; and 'Sur l'application du droit du travail et de l'emploi au-delà du contrat du travail' (2007) 146 *Revue International du Travail* 3 ff.

taken up by the *Employment in Europe 2010* report,[13] which noted that the financial and economic crisis that began in 2008 has highlighted the flaws of a policy strategy that fosters employment growth almost exclusively through the development of temporary and other forms of 'atypical' contracts. Such strategies increase employment volatility and jeopardize sustainable economic growth; hence the importance of proposing alternative policies that will create stable jobs – for example, by introducing fiscal incentives for enterprises to hire permanent workers and convert temporary contracts into permanent (or open-ended) ones.[14]

In the conclusions and proposals presented in *Employment in Europe 2010*, the Commission draws attention to the various measures proposed by influential economists, including the adoption of a 'single permanent contract' to sweep away the existing legal asymmetry between the permanent and the fixed-term contract. A new contract of this kind would offer increased security of tenure (for example, through a gradual rise in severance payments), entitlement to a minimum wage and universal eligibility for unemployment insurance, while the use of temporary contracts would be limited to certain specific circumstances, such as genuinely temporary tasks or highly paid work.

Thus defined, the single employment contract increases protection for workers while also fostering social mobility, and introduces the concept of professional status, as highlighted in the Supiot Report (Supiot, 1999). According to this concept, the optimal level of job security requires the identification of a new worker as embarking both on an individual career within the enterprise and a professional career over a working lifetime that is likely to involve mobility between work of varying types and durations. In this context, the main task of labour law, until such career mobility is fully attained, would be to ensure stability of employment (not of any one job), thereby maintaining the worker's status and recognizing their continuing social rights, which need to be redesigned within a new social security vision.

In this way, the single employment contract addresses the key issues on which criticism has been levelled at the flexicurity model.[15] Irrespective of the long-standing dispute about the impact of employment protection legislation (EPL) on unemployment levels, if the liberalization of dismissal procedures is not accompanied by market conditions that can absorb workers within their 'life cycle', the effectiveness of the flexicurity model will continue to be questioned.

These concerns are borne out by research on unemployment rates carried out between March 2008 and March 2010. While this research shows that countries that have taken the flexicurity route tend to have lower overall unemployment rates than other countries, and lower female unemployment, youth unemployment in these countries has increased.[16] It should also be noted that both non-flexicurity countries

---

13 See: ec.europa.eu/employment_social/eie/executive_summarys_en.html.

14 The terms 'permanent' and 'open-ended' are used interchangeably in this context.

15 See Auer, P, 'Security in Labour Markets: Combining Flexibility with Security for Decent Work' (2007) Economic and Labour Market Papers 12 (Geneva, ILO).

16 See Kongshøj Madsen, P, 'Reagire alla tempesta. La flexicurity danese e la crisi' (2011) 21(1) *Diritto delle Relazioni Industriali* 78. Denmark is the country where unemployment was increased both in absolute and relative terms when compared with other countries.

and flexicurity countries have made only marginal use of layoffs in responding to the recent crisis, tending to prefer the reduction of working hours. In Germany, for example, the balanced management of the 'bank of hours' before and during the crisis, with extensive use of short-time working (*Kurzarbeit*), is believed to have avoided the loss of 1.2 million jobs between 2008 and 2009. The German Government also encouraged the use of training rather than layoffs, with the public employment service continuing to pay both training and social security costs. This strategy was a win–win solution.

The approach taken by Germany and certain other European countries, combining higher employment protection with subsidized domestic measures, differs from the Danish flexicurity model, which is characterized by limited employment protection accompanied by substantial measures to support the unemployed. The former route certainly incurred higher costs for enterprises, but in the long run these were outweighed by the economic gains. Consequently, it is no surprise that the European leaders most praised for their management of the crisis were those who focused on keeping people in jobs, where possible through providing support to businesses with the introduction of flexible working models and temporary adjustments, including alternative forms of internal flexibility – all to the ultimate end of mitigating the social impacts of the crisis and preventing companies from losing skilled human capital.[17]

The idea of the single employment contract merits an investigation that starts from the debate that surrounded its genesis and moves on to evaluate the pros and cons of the proposal in the context of current labour market problems. The comparative analysis presented here will provide useful information by which both the virtues of the single employment contract and the contradictions inherent in the idea can be considered and assessed.

We begin by setting out the general framework within which the current debate developed by outlining the origins of the problem that gave rise to the proposal of a single employment contract. We then move on to review the debate on labour market segmentation and the flexicurity proposal. From there we go on to examine the basis of the single employment contract, certain of its key characteristics and the major arguments put forward both for and against it. Brief case studies are then presented of how the idea has been taken forward in Italy, France and Spain. There follows a concise review of contractual arrangements in EU labour markets before a concluding section on future projections and possible developments.

[17] Council of the European Union, 'Flexicurity in times of crisis' European Council Resolution (2009) 2.

Flexibility 1

1.1 The Origins of the Issue: The Demand for Labour Market Flexibility

Over the three decades since the 1980s, labour law has been challenged by the demand for flexibility, which has altered the traditional structure of the labour market and continues to act as a powerful driver for change.

In post-industrial societies, under the pressures of globalization and international competition, the labour market has seen a legal and institutional response to the growing need of enterprises for flexibility in production and organization, with repercussions for individuals in respect of changes to the framework of employment and social rights.

The paradigm that has dominated labour markets since the 1980s has been that of organizational flexibility at work. This term 'flexibility' derives from the Latin *flectere* (to bend). What can be bent is flexible and, by extension, can be adapted to different conditions. The term 'job', in the context of work, originally meant a 'block' or a 'piece', something that could be physically moved from one place to another. As Richard Sennett reminds us, flexible capitalism is reinstating this archaic meaning of 'job', and thereby is changing the very meaning of work: people who work no longer follow a 'career' (channelling their efforts in a particular direction which they will follow throughout their working life), but have to perform discrete 'pieces' of work in a sequence of possibly unconnected tasks.[1]

In this 'liquid' post-modernity – so called in order to oppose it to the 'compact and solid' modernity represented by the Fordist factory – work becomes an archipelago of activities conforming to the model of contingent work as defined by Matusik and Hill.[2]

[1] Sennett, R, *The Corrosion of Character: The Personal Consequences of The New Capitalism* (New York, Norton, 1998)

[2] To summarize: 'contingent workforce consists of independent contractors; individuals brought in through employment agencies; on-call or day labour; and workers on site whose services are provided by contract firms,

In the theoretical literature, the elements of uncertainty and risk are identified as disrupting social patterns based on traditional values, marking an irreversible discontinuity between twentieth-century capitalism and contemporary forms of production and social organization.

A state of endemic uncertainty characterizes the lives and the means of subsistence of the majority of human beings today. In the field of work, new elements of uncertainty, instability and unpredictability combine with the fear that the very process of industrialization and the concomitant extensive network of public instruments developed by the West during the twentieth century are gradually being eroded, even to the point of abolition. This is an irreversible process, reflecting profound changes in economic and social structures. The more critical analyses tell us that post-Fordism incorporates in its productive paradigm a new 'polytheism of work'.[3] While the Fordist model was based on a relatively homogeneous labour market, compatible with the pursuit of full employment, and on a production system based on the prevalence of mass production in basic industries, which tended to create stable (albeit not fully rewarding) working conditions for most of those employed, the model of the post-Fordist society provides us, on the one hand, with a highly segmented labour market, where unemployment and job insecurity tend to be structural and, on the other, with a production system that responds to differentiated and personalized needs.

This new model embodies the explicit recognition of new heterogeneous and heterodox types of work, in many cases not adequately supported (as for example where national programmes for youth employment are not backed up with sufficient public funding), and characterized by instability and flexibility. Labour market structures are weak, compared with the Fordist era. The employee is constantly placed on the border that separates the universe of stable guarantees from that of precarious or informal work: a nomadic figure, moving between the area of work and that of non-work.

In this new Olympus, the presiding deity of work is no longer the blacksmith Hephaestus who ruled in the late nineteenth-century but Proteus, god of change and instability; as one writer has put it, adaptability has taken the place of regularity as a theological virtue.[4] The consequences of these processes are summarized in the recognition that 'the stable, full-time and permanent contract is no longer the lodestar of labour law'.[5]

According to the established model of organizational flexibility, the enterprise is structured around a core and a periphery.[6] In the core, we find the most qualified workers, who represent a source of knowledge and experience that defines the identity of the organization (its core business) and strengthens the enterprise; in the periphery we find the least skilled workforce.

---

such as outsourced information technology workers', see Matusik, SF and Hill, CWL, 'The Utilization of Contingent Work, Knowledge Creation, and Competitive Advantage' (1998) 23(4) *Academy of Management Review* 680.

[3] Perulli, A, 'Il diritto del lavoro tra libertà e sicurezza' (2012) 31(2) *Rivista Italiana di Diritto del Lavoro* 247 ff.

[4] Revelli, M, *Oltre il novecento. La politica, le ideologie e le insidie del lavoro* (Torino, Einaudi, 2001).

[5] Ghezzi, G and Romagnoli, U, *Il rapporto di lavoro* 3rd edn (Bologna, Zanichelli, 1995).

[6] See Atkinson, JG, 'Manpower Strategies for Flexible Organizations' (1984) 16(8) *Personnel Management* 28 ff.

An enterprise that focuses on its core business seeks long-term contracts, setting itself the goal of retaining its employees in the internal labour market, especially in areas of close to full employment, in innovative sectors, and in areas of the new economy that call for highly specialized professionals who are in short supply.[7] In this environment, flexibility is likely to take functional form, while workers are more often subject to numerical flexibility.[8] In this context, too, enterprises routinely use the open-ended employment contract, in part because of the collective goods that are connected with these contracts – for example, the skills and cooperation built up within the enterprise.[9]

1.2 Different Kinds of Flexibility

'Flexibility', as applied to labour markets, can mean different things in different contexts, and can result from a variety of factors. The economic and sociological literature identifies, in addition to matters related to systems of labour regulation, taxation and social welfare, factors related to both the demand for labour (including fluctuations of the economic cycle, the kinds of technology used and the characteristics of production systems), and the supply of labour (such as education levels, family composition and demographic structure).

The greatest impetus for labour flexibility comes from the enterprise, reflecting the imperatives of production and organization (personalization of products for consumers, production on demand, rapid response times, etc). The management literature emphasizes the importance of flexible working patterns in order to ensure competitiveness, recognizing the flexible enterprise as the model best suited to exploit new market opportunities.[10] The flexible enterprise needs workers who are not only skilled but also adaptable, and a labour market that guarantees external (or numerical) flexibility and internal (or functional) flexibility as well as wage flexibility.

Enterprises can in principle choose between internal and external flexibility, and the experience of many systems shows a trade-off between the two types of flexibility, or between flexibility and employment security. A good example is Japan in the 1980s, where the trade-off was between job security (avoiding resort to external flexibility) on the one hand and, on the other, the ability to adapt quickly in the organization of work (extensive use of functional or internal flexibility), often involving changes in working time and tasks.

[7] See Altuzarra, A and Serrano, F, 'Firms' Innovation Activity and Numerical Flexibility' (2010) 63(2) *Industrial and Labor Relations Review* 327 ff.

[8] On the distinction between numerical flexibility and functional flexibility see the next section.

[9] See Altuzarra and Serrano, above (n 7) which described a non-linear relationship between flexibility and innovative enterprises.

[10] See Atkinson, above (n 6) and Hunter, L, McGregor, A, MacInnes, J and Sproull, A, 'The "Flexible Firm": Strategy and Segmentation' (1993) 31(2) *British Journal of Industrial Relations* 383 ff.

The enterprise has a large toolkit at its disposal in pursuing the goal of numerical flexibility in the workforce, including both standard and atypical contracts. Its use of these various arrangements will vary to suit its own operational and organizational context, taking account of the local environment, the economic sector, the size of the enterprise and the characteristics of the workforce available in that particular market. Each type of employment contract responds to a specific organizational, production or strategic need of the enterprise. It is often assumed that atypical contracts are underused owing to legislative inadequacies, or, conversely, that they are over-used because too much protection is attached to the standard contract. However, some empirical studies reject both these assumptions.[11]

While numerical or external flexibility concerns the dynamics of the external labour market, flexibility in wages and working time (instances of internal flexibility) affects the internal labour market. External flexibility concerns the employer's ability to move a workplace to another location or change the goods or services produced – in both cases exploiting this flexibility through the exercise of the managerial authority vested in him or her as employer.[12] Internal flexibility, by contrast, concerns the degree of freedom the enterprise has to adjust the volume and the professional characteristics of the workforce in line with the development of production and technological changes.

Although, in principle, enterprises are free to choose which kind of flexibility they prefer, in practice they are subject to some constraints in the form of labour market regulations, the guidance of regulatory systems in the matters of hiring and firing and customs and practices of industrial relations that govern the 'adjustments' made between internal and external flexibility.

These business practices may include, for example, a preference for wage flexibility through the use of variable pay rather than dismissal (as in Japan), or for functional/internal flexibility, supported by the use of short-time working, as in Germany, where 80 per cent of adjustments to accommodate changes in the production cycle are implemented using internal flexibility, above all the *Kurzarbeit* scheme.[13] In other contexts, such as the United States, the preferred option is external/numerical flexibility.[14]

In recent years, external or numerical flexibility seems to have become the privileged form, taking priority over the internal or qualitative form. However, despite the fact that numerical flexibility dominates the European debate on the efficiency of the labour market, one should not underestimate the need for functional flexibility, as expressed by the most innovative among medium and large enterprises.[15]

---

[11] Esping-Andersen, G and Regini, M (eds), *Why Deregulate Labour Markets?* (Oxford, Oxford University Press, 2000).

[12] Perulli, A, *Il potere direttivo dell'imprenditore* (Milano, Giuffrè, 1992).

[13] See Hohendanner, C and Bellman, L, 'Interne und externe Flexibilität' (2006) 5 *WSI Mitteilungen.*

[14] See Abraham, KG and Houseman, SN, 'Labor Adjustment under Different Institutional Structures: A Case Study of Germany and the United States' in F Buttler, W Franz, R Schettkat and D Soskice (eds), *Institutional Frameworks and Labor Market Performance: Comparative Views on the US and German Economies* (London, Routledge, 1995).

[15] See Barbieri, P, 'Lavoro flessibile e disuguaglianze in Europa' (2009) 25 *European Sociological Review* 621 ff.

Nonetheless, in the current economic and legal debate numerical flexibility is considered the essential prerequisite for the proper functioning of the labour market. There are three main strands to this type of flexibility: (a) regulatory, legal or conventional constraints governing hiring and firing (so-called incoming and outgoing flexibility); (b) the possibility of using atypical employment relationships, structurally different from permanent, full-time contracts; and (c) the tendency to outsource or contract out phases or functions within the production cycle to other businesses, to domestic workers, or to external partners through self-employment contracts.

As well as these three elements, other features of an emphasis on numerical flexibility include, first, the maintenance of a certain rigidity in the functional profile of the enterprise; second, the dependence of a fixed core of workers with open-ended contracts on the presence of a variable periphery of contingent workers, whose contribution is gained through the use of atypical contracts; and third, the use of atypical arrangements not only in respect of contracts of employment, but also in different ways of negotiating links among enterprises that perform many forms of outsourcing in the allocation and management of work.[16]

1.3 From the Standard Employment Contract to a Plurality of Types

With the adoption of numerical flexibility as a key principle in the labour market, terms such as 'flexible working arrangements' and 'atypical contracts' have become part of the DNA of the new labour law. These ideas have been adopted with a view to representing those forms of working relationship not captured by the model of 'standard' work, characterized by a permanent full-time employment contract between employer and employee. The addition of extra provisions to the employment relationship or the removal of existing ones has involved departures from legal norms, usually weakening the protection system typical of the standard employment model.[17]

The Fordist model of production and consumption, based on mass production and economies of scale, required the provision of stable, standardized and regulated working conditions. In employment terms, this model was based on the 'Fordist compromise', whereby workers accepted subordination in exchange for stability/continuity of employment. Labour law in European countries was built on a regulatory model tailored to this standard model, all deviations from which were classified as exceptional, atypical or non-standard forms.

[16] See Barbera, M, 'Trasformazioni della figura del datore di lavoro e flessibilizzazione delle regole del diritto' (2010) 32 *Giornale di diritto del lavoro e di relazioni industriali* 203 ff.

[17] Santoro-Passarelli, G, 'Competitività e flessibilità del rapporto di lavoro' (2009) I *Rivista Italiana di Diritto del Lavoro* 206.

This employment relationship model began to enter into crisis in the 1980s, driven by the need for flexibility in an economic system making the transition from Fordism to post-Fordism. Flexibility was presented as a response to the critical situation of the labour market, extrinsic to the paradigm of labour law and not involving the deregulation of the employment relationship or the dismantling of the legislation supporting trade unionism.[18]

At this point, the rules and regulations governing enterprises tended to diminish. Enhancement of skills took place within the enterprise, and in the European and Japanese contexts social mobility too was concentrated within the enterprise, with career progression 'in place'; in the American context, by contrast, social mobility occurred predominantly by movement from one employer to another.

In the subsequent two decades, the widely accepted need for flexibility was combined with the organizational imperative of fighting unemployment. In this context, the potential for non-standard jobs seemed to represent an incentive to create new jobs – a view encapsulated in the slogan 'more flexibility, less unemployment'.

Some commentators took the view that flexibility was promoted by an ideological impetus;[19] others, that it was dictated by rational choices aimed at reducing the duration of unemployment and the high turnover of those in jobs.[20] Either way, the interest in improving employability that emerged alongside the principle of flexibility has helped to change the perceived function of labour law, now envisaged as providing a set of technical regulations conducive to matching labour demand and supply.

These requirements of 'flexible employment' have been accompanied in many European countries by active measures on the part of national legislators to reform existing laws, as well as by a new acceptance by organizations of new forms of employment different from that long considered the standard.[21] Today, 'non-standard' or 'atypical' work is becoming more familiar. Indeed, with some significant exceptions, non-standard work is less and less 'atypical', so that the terminology is no longer appropriate: it is estimated that almost 50 per cent of the entire workforce in the European Union is now engaged in non-standard work of one form or another.[22]

This trend is exemplified by the case of Italy, where a fragmentation of working arrangements has been translated into a multitude of flexible forms of employment

[18] Flexibility as 'necessary evil' as written by Caruso, B, 'Flexible Working Time: The Italian Case' in Caruso, B and Fuchs, M (eds), *Labour Law and Flexibility in Europe: The Cases of Germany and Italy* (Baden-Baden, Nomos; Milano, Giuffrè, 2004) 19.

[19] See ibid.

[20] See Blanchard, O, *La disoccupazione in Europa: il ruolo degli shock e delle istituzioni* (Roma, Banca d'Italia Edizioni dell'Elefante, 1999) 96 ff.

[21] See Hamandia, A, 'Germany: Towards a Dual Labour Market?' in F Eyraud and D Vaughan-Whitehead, *The Evolving World of Work in the Enlarged EU: Progress and Vulnerability* (Geneva, ILO, 2007) 269 ff; Nacsa, B and Köllo, J, 'Hungary: Employment Instability due to Fixed-Term Contracts' in Eyraud and Vaughan-Whitehead, ibid, 319 ff; Muñoz De Bustillo Llorente, R, 'Spain: The Paradox of Job Insecurity Alongside High Employment Growth' in Eyraud and Vaughan-Whitehead, ibid, 439 ff; Lundberg, J and Cronberg, E, 'Sweden: From Permanent to Temporary Employment Relationships' in Eyraud and Vaughan-Whitehead, ibid, 481 ff; Grimshaw, D and Marchington, L, 'United Kingdom: Persistent inequality and vulnerability traps' in Eyraud and Vaughan-Whitehead, ibid, 517 ff.

[22] More precisely, 48.5 per cent, according to the Employment in Europe, 2006 Statistical Annex.

contracts. Provisions for flexibility in the most recent legislation (in particular the Biagi Law, Legislative Decree no 276/2003) resulted in a proliferation of schemes as alternatives to the standard employment contract, although in this case the positive approach to flexibility was justified in terms of the aim of combating fraudulent or openly illegal forms of employment.[23] This kind of flexibility reflects a highly segmented labour market in which large groups of workers remain outside the production system, confined in conditions of precariousness, as reflected in low levels of social protection, lack of investment in training, poor continuity of employment and lack of access to paths for professional growth.[24]

In parallel to the spread of non-standard jobs in subordinate employment, labour markets are witnessing an increase in new forms of activity that challenge the traditional distinction, characteristic of all European juridical systems, between dependent employment and self-employment. The hypothesis put forward in the literature is that the evolution of methods of production and organization, with widespread disaggregation of enterprises and use of outsourcing, has mobilized a new generation of self-employed who maintain an organizational coordination with the enterprise and a strong economic dependence upon it.[25] The crisis of the traditional dichotomy between employment and self-employment, a source of unequal treatment that appears less and less justifiable, suggests that it is necessary to redefine the qualifying criteria for self-employment and re-examine the relative protections given to the employed and self-employed. In their different ways, the Italian debate on the need for a 'reshaping of safeguards', the hypothesis of a *tertium genus* between employment and self-employment,[26] the proposal for an extended range of degrees of subordination through the creation of a contract for working 'on behalf of others'[27] and suggestions in important segments of proposed European legislation and regulation dealing with the distinction between self-employment and economically dependent work,[28] are all significant elements of this process of critically revisiting the traditional categories.

---

[23] See report on Legislative Decree no. 276/2003.

[24] See Ghezzi, G, 'Dove va il diritto del lavoro? Afferrare Proteo' (2002) 3 *Lavoro e Diritto* 333 ff; Mariucci, L, 'La forza di un pensiero debole. Una critica del Libro Bianco del lavoro' (2002) 1 *Lavoro e Diritto* 3 ff; Alleva, PG, Andreoni, A, Angiolini, V, Coccia, F and Naccari, G, 'La delega al Governo per il mercato del lavoro: un disegno autoritario nel metodo, eversivo nei contenuti' in P Alleva et al, *Lavoro, ritorno al passato – Critica del Libro Bianco e della legge delega al Governo Berlusconi sul mercato del lavoro* (Roma, Ediesse, 2002) 69 ff.; Pinto, V and Voza, R, 'Il Governo Berlusconi e il diritto del lavoro: dal libro bianco al disegno di legge delega' (2002) I *Rivista Giuridica del Lavoro e della Previdenza Sociale* 454 ff.

[25] Perulli, A, *Economically Dependent/Quasi-subordinate (Parasubordinate) Employment: Legal, Social and Economic Aspects* (Brussels, European Commission, 2003).

[26] *cf* De Luca Tamajo, VR, 'Per una revisione delle categorie qualificatorie del diritto del lavoro: l'emersione del lavoro coordinato' (1997) 5 *Argomenti di Diritto del Lavoro* 41 ff, and Perulli, A, 'Lavoro coordinato' *Digesto, disc* priv – sez comm, (Torino, Agg., 2000).

[27] *cf* Perulli, A, 'Il diritto del lavoro fra crisi della subordinazione e rinascita del lavoro autonomo' (1997) 2 *Lavoro e Diritto* 173 ff; Pedrazzoli, M, 'Dai lavori autonomi ai lavori subordinati' in G Giugni (ed), *Scritti in onore di Gino Giugni* (Bari, Cacucci, 1999).

[28] *cf* Perulli, A, 'Lavoro autonomo e dipendenza economica, oggi' (2003) I *Rivista Giuridica del Lavoro* 221 ff; Perulli, A, 'Per uno statuto del lavoro autonomo' (2010) 3 *Diritto delle Relazioni Industriali* 621 ff.

Segmentation 2

2.1 Segmentation in EU Labour Markets

In recent years, labour markets in several European Union Member States have been characterized by increasing dualism or segmentation. Segmentation of labour markets describes the situation when there are 'various sub-groups which have little crossover capability'.[1] Dualism describes the particular case where some workers have stable employment relationships and others work under temporary employment contracts, often trapped in temporary jobs[2] without much probability of moving into a long-term employment relationship.

Segmented labour markets give rise to concerns, both from a social and from an economic point of view. In social terms, segmentation may have negative effects on equity, career development, self-esteem and also productivity. Workers who move from one temporary job to another have discontinuous careers characterized by long spells of unemployment, lower wages (14 per cent lower than permanent workers on average, all other things being equal) and lower national insurance contributions. These facts call for a serious debate on the long-term repercussions for both employment and wages.

Segmentation considerably increases labour market volatility, with temporary workers bearing the brunt of adjustment. The Organisation for Economic Co-operation and Development (2009)[3] found that the rising share of temporary contracts has been responsible for an increase of almost 9 per cent in the volatility of total hours worked across the business cycle in OECD countries (the volatility for temporary workers is about 2.5 times as high as for permanent ones). Overall, the changing balance between temporary and permanent contracts contributed substantially to the improvement in the EU labour market before the crisis that began in 2008. However, the corollary is a higher level of job losses during times of recession, concentrated in workers on temporary contracts, who are mainly young and low-skilled. Indeed, compared with 2008, numbers of permanent jobs have fallen

1 See Wilkinson, F, *The Dynamics of Labour Market Segmentation* (London, Academic Press, 1981).

2 See *Employment in Europe* (2010) ch 3 at: ec.europa.eu/social/main.jsp?catId=738&langId=en&pubId=593.

3 See: www.oecd.org/employment/database.

more for young workers (down by 14 per cent) than for prime-age workers (down by 4 per cent), while increasing for older workers (up by 2.5 per cent).[4]

The disproportionate share of adjustment falling on temporary contracts can lead to higher real wage rigidity, that is, less response of wages to unemployment levels. Indeed, workers on permanent contracts, if not directly affected by a recession, can more easily disregard the interests of those in temporary contracts,[5] leading to higher unemployment among the latter.

Workers employed on temporary contracts, or work for agencies or on other forms of short-term contracts, often receive less on-the-job training, thus reducing productivity. They also tend to have more accidents at work,[6] and to be subject to more credit constraints.[7]

Arguably the most serious problem associated with dualism in the labour market, however, is the likely effect on future pension rights, owing to the functioning of the labour market itself (lower earnings, frequent breaks and weak unemployment insurance) rather than to the rules applying to pension schemes. It is estimated that non-permanent contract workers will have pensions lower than permanent workers – by 59 per cent in Italy and 56 per cent in Sweden.

Labour market segmentation particularly affects young people accessing the labour market for the first time or having recently entered it, and low-skilled workers looking for new jobs after a period of unemployment. One of the major causes of segmentation lies in the reforms undertaken in European labour markets in the 1980s and 1990s to boost flexibility in order to increase enterprises' productivity and workers' employability. At this time, both academics and international organizations were blaming excessively stringent legislation governing the dismissal of workers as a contributory cause of high unemployment rates in several countries.[8] In response to this pressure, many governments did indeed change employment protection legislation (EPL). However, in many cases, political considerations prevented governments from relaxing EPL right across the labour market, so that regulations were changed for only certain segments of the working population, and reducing EPL only for new entrants often appeared to be the easiest strategy. Indeed, in most countries, EPL for workers employed under standard contracts remained almost unchanged between 1990 and 2008, while regulations for temporary workers have been considerably eased over the same period. EPL has been strengthened for temporary workers only in those countries that started from the lowest levels. In particular, the scope of temporary contracts was significantly expanded, and temporary agency work became more widespread.

[4] Perulli, A, 'Il diritto del lavoro tra libertà e sicurezza' (2012) 31(2) *Rivista Italiana di Diritto del Lavoro* 247.

[5] See Bentolila, S and Dolado, J, 'Labour Flexibility and Wages: Lessons from Spain' (1994) 18 *Economic Policy* 53.

[6] See Guadalupe, M, 'The Hidden Costs of Fixed-term Contracts: The Impact on Work Accidents' (2003) 10 *Labour Economics* 339; Boeri, T and Galasso, V, 'Is Social Security Secure with NDC?' (2010) IZA Discussion Paper Series No 5235.

[7] See Barceló, C and Villanueva, E, 'The Response of Household Wealth to the Risk of Losing the Job: Evidence from Differences in Firing Costs' (2010) Banco de España, Working Paper No 1002.

[8] Ibid.

Certainly, temporary contracts are not in themselves problematic; indeed, they play a productive role in labour markets, providing enterprises with the flexibility they need in planning their production processes and workers with a route into more secure contracts. However, because in many circumstances the costs to enterprises associated with temporary contracts were far lower than those attached to open-ended contracts an incentive existed for employers to make a disproportionate use of the former even where production needs would have justified the recruitment of permanent workers. In some countries, fixed-term contracts were also used under the guise of forms of self-employment.[9]

Through the Europe 2020 flagship initiatives 'Youth on the Move' and 'An Agenda for New Skills and Jobs', both launched in 2010, the European Commission opened a debate on the introduction of single open-ended contracts or an extended use of open-ended contracts in highly segmented labour markets, not only, but principally, for young workers aged between 15 and 29 – the age cohort for which temporary contracts are more widely used than for any other in the EU is 27. The intention behind the proposal was to explore new forms of contractual arrangements to reduce segmentation and create a more uniform labour market based on flexicurity principles.

The Commission presented some proposals at an informal meeting in Budapest on 5–6 April 2011. On that occasion, delegates raised several issues calling for further reflection and analytical underpinning:

- Are contractual arrangements a source of labour market segmentation?
- What are the different contractual arrangements available in each European Union country? And how do these respond to the pressing call for more labour market flexibility?
- How would a single employment contract connect with policies in other areas such as wages, social protection systems (ie, unemployment benefits) and lifelong learning?
- Who would be affected by the single employment contract – who are the end recipients?

Answers to these questions will help to establish a better understanding of the situation in European labour markets and enable more informed judgements to be made on optimal solutions and their eventual application. The focus here will be mainly on the first question.

[9] See Casale, G (ed), *The Employment Relationship: A Comparative Overview* (Oxford, Hart Publishing; ILO, Geneva, 2011).

2.2 Contractual Arrangements and Segmentation in EU Labour Markets

Segmentation of labour markets can refer to divisions between genders, sectors, regions or skill groups. Here we focus on segmentation arising from differences in contractual arrangements: specifically, the division between workers with stable employment relationships and other workers with temporary employment contracts.

As noted above, changes in EPL across EU Member States aimed mainly at easing regulations governing temporary work have been accompanied by an increase in the proportion of temporary workers, both in the entire workforce and among young people in particular. There is, indeed, a positive and significant correlation between the change in the relative strictness of EPL applying to permanent and temporary contracts, and the share of temporary workers in the labour force.

With some reservations, the EPL indicator is very useful for identifying rigidities on the exit side of the labour market, that is, regulation of dismissals. The OECD has collected information from its Member States on notice periods and severance pay after 9 months, 4 years, and 20 years of employment.[10] However, the EPL indicator offers no information on the functioning of contractual arrangements on the entry side of the market or on the way in which protection rights, both legal and monetary, are built up at the beginning of the working career. This type of information is not easily available for EU countries either; and yet it is fundamental in evaluating the impact of contractual arrangements on labour market segmentation and therefore in designing reforms aimed at facilitating smooth and steady entry into the labour market.

2.2.1 The Prominence of Young People among Temporary Workers

It has been noted above that young people are disproportionately strongly represented among temporary workers. While this pattern is evident in nearly all EU Member States, the ratio of temporary to permanent contracts varies considerably among countries. In some Member States, temporary contracts account for almost all contracts for very young workers (15–18 years old). However, this group has a low participation in the labour market, and so it is more productive to focus on workers aged 19 and above.

In all EU Member States the use of temporary contracts decreases with age, but still accounts for over half of all employees until about 30 years of age. Spain, Portugal and Poland show a considerably and persistently higher share of temporary workers compared with other Member States. In Germany, France and Sweden, the age profile is much steeper, meaning that temporary contracts are more strongly concentrated on

[10] www.oecd.org/dataoecd/24/39/42740165.pdf.

young workers, the proportion diminishing quickly with age. Most of the new Member States (notably Bulgaria, Estonia, Hungary, Latvia, Lithuania, Romania, Slovakia and Malta), plus the United Kingdom and Ireland, show a low total share of temporary workers but a flatter pattern across the age spectrum: that is, temporary contracts are used less frequently and spread more evenly across workers of all ages.

2.2.2 The Missing Transition to Permanent Contracts

Viewing the situation at a single point in time does not, however, show the whole picture. If attention is focused on new contracts the dynamics of the situation become much clearer. More than 80 per cent of new contracts signed in Spain in the last decade, for example, are temporary. The figure is almost as high – around 70 per cent – in Slovenia, Portugal and Poland; and in Sweden, France, Germany, Finland, the Netherlands and Italy, 50 per cent or more hirings are arranged on a fixed-term basis. If this pattern persists, even those countries that now seem to have a relatively lower share of temporary workers (such as Italy, Greece, Belgium and Luxembourg) will soon see the proportion increase steeply as permanent workers exit the labour market and around 40–50 per cent of new hirings are made on temporary contracts.

As noted above, entering the labour market via a temporary contract is not necessarily a bad thing. For a young person, for example, it may represent the easiest way to gain some experience and enrich one's CV while keeping open the option of changing job to exploit better opportunities. However, as the use of temporary contracts has expanded, so the chances of moving from a temporary contract to an open-ended contract have diminished. While in some EU Member States (observed before the economic crisis of 2008) a temporary contract worker had a good chance of moving into a permanent contract after a period of one year or in some countries even longer, workers in France, Portugal, Cyprus, Greece, Finland, Poland, Spain, Italy, the Czech Republic, Belgium, Luxembourg, Lithuania and Slovenia all have less than a 50 per cent chance of moving into a permanent contract after one year of temporary work. In these cases it is clear that segmentation applies.

When the data are disaggregated by country and age group, further distinctions appear. It becomes apparent that young people find it especially hard to make the transition to permanent contracts in Slovenia and Spain; conversely, in Hungary and Belgium, despite a general difficulty in moving from temporary to permanent jobs, young people are more likely to make the transition. In the United Kingdom, older workers find it difficult to move from temporary into permanent work, and the same pattern can be seen in Lithuania, Ireland, Austria, the Czech Republic and Cyprus. Thus temporary contracts may not only fail to represent a reliable entry point into the permanent labour force for young people, but can also trap older workers. In yet another group of EU Member States, including Sweden, Italy, Poland, Finland, Greece, Portugal and France, there appears to be no strong correlation between age and the likelihood of moving into a permanent contract.

One question we should ask here is: to what extent are these patterns related to skills and education? Are people locked in temporary employment contracts simply because they lack the right skills to find permanent jobs?

In general, higher levels of skill attainment help to increase the probability of moving from a temporary contract to a permanent contract in France (though only very slightly), Finland and Poland, and to some extent also in Greece and Slovakia. However, in other countries, for example the Czech Republic, the trend is reversed, so that the higher the education level the lower the probability of moving from a temporary contract to a permanent contract. In some other EU Member States, secondary education considerably increases the likelihood of moving from a temporary to a permanent job: this is the case in Sweden, Belgium, Hungary, Austria and Latvia. And in yet others, such as Italy, there is no clear pattern. Overall, the returns on education in terms of 'job security' are very low.[11]

2.2.3 The Consequences of Labour Market Segmentation

As noted above, segmented labour markets give rise to concerns from both the social and the economic point of view. The lower overall wages and lower work intensity characteristic of a segmented labour market are a source of in-work poverty, which affects 13 per cent of those on temporary contracts and just 5 per cent of those on permanent contracts.[12]

Temporary and permanent contracts respond differently to business cycle fluctuations, with temporary employment responding at least twice as strongly as the overall employment response to changes in GDP. What this means in practice is that job losses during recessions are concentrated on those with temporary contracts, that is, mostly young people and low-skilled workers.

The disproportionate share of adjustment falling on temporary contracts can lead to higher real wage rigidity. 'Insiders' are not only insulated from unemployment but may also profit from a two-tier labour market. In Spain in 2009 the construction sector shed one quarter (23 per cent) of its labour force, but wages increased by 3.9 per cent, benefiting those who kept their jobs. Workers who have temporary contracts, or work for temporary agencies or on other forms of short contracts, often receive less on-the-job training, thus reducing productivity.

Fighting segmentation is becoming a priority to address not only the short-term challenges in terms of individual career paths but also the long-term imperatives of improved productivity, investment in human capital and adequate pension provision.

---

[11] The analysis at this stage cannot make distinctions based on the type of education (in particular types of tertiary degrees, professional education versus general diploma, etc) or its quality; nevertheless, it confirms that contractual segmentation is not (or not only) attributable to poor skills and education.

[12] Figures for the EU. For a more in-depth discussion on the link between segmentation and in-work poverty, see the Synthesis Report by the EU Network of Independent Experts on Social Inclusion: 'In-Work Poverty and Labour Market: Segmentation in the EU: Key Lessons' at: http: www.peer-review-social-inclusion.eu/network-of-independent-experts/reports/2010-second-semester/synthesis-report_2_2010_en.

2.2.4 Where Do We Go from Here?

One possible but politically infeasible way of solving segmentation would be simply to phase out temporary contracts. However, moving back to the labour market of some decades ago, where only open-ended contracts were available, would probably lead to the worst of all possible outcomes: large job losses during a downturn and poor job creation during a subsequent recovery.

What is needed now is smarter regulation, adapted to the needs of the countries with segmented labour markets and tailored to respect industrial relations traditions, to pave the way to a recovery rich in 'decent work' and on to a better balance between flexibility and protection in good times. In particular, these new forms of labour regulation need to offer enterprises a viable alternative to the over-use of temporary contracts.

It was mainly in response to this imperative that the European Commission opened a debate on the introduction of single employment contracts, or an extended use of open-ended contracts, in highly segmented labour markets. The single employment contract would sweep away many of the existing discontinuities between contractual arrangements and enable transitions to be made more easily from one type of work to another. Moreover, where fixed-term contracts are used, neither the worker nor the enterprise generally has much incentive to make productivity-enhancing job-specific investments. If these employment relations were replaced by the single employment contract, the uncertainty associated with temporary contracts would be reduced, creating incentives on both sides of the relationship to make these types of investment, thereby stimulating productivity.

Reforms in contractual arrangements alone will not solve the problems associated with segmentation. These types of reforms will need to be consistent with, and create synergies with, other key pillars of labour market policy: active labour market policies, social security systems and lifelong learning.

The Single Employment Contract: Origins and Presuppositions 3

3.1 The Origins of the Single Employment Contract: 'Re-Thinking' Work

Organizational models based on flexible production inevitably call for the adoption of contractual arrangements under which work is temporary or in other ways precarious. Numerical flexibility, in particular, allows the enterprise to change its number of employees following the production cycle, ideally in real time, or at least with minimal delay. To meet these demands, the standard employment contract needs to be supported by other types of contractual arrangements.[1] What these 'atypical' arrangements usually have in common is a lightening of the legal constraints that usually characterize the standard employment contract. The related transformations of labour law in various national contexts have involved a diversification of the legal conditions governing work and the emergence of a new kind of regulation which calls into question some key traditional principles, including the social integration, that is a key pillar of the labour law system.[2]

In the Italian case, this process has been effected through a series of incremental measures which have gradually introduced numerical flexibility without accompanying corrections in the welfare system to compensate for the loss of security in the labour market.

Under the 'Biagi law' which reformed the labour market (Legislative Decree no. 276/2003), the extension of the flexibility available under existing types of contracts was augmented by the creation of additional types of flexible contract, covering both subordinate employment (facilitating, for example, intermittent work, work on call, staff leasing and occasional and accessory work), and self-employment (for example, project work).[3] These types of flexible contract also feature a variety

[1] D'Antona, M (ed), *Politiche di flessibilità e mutamenti del diritto del lavoro: Italia e Spagna* (Napoli, Esi, 1990) 12.

[2] Supiot, A, *Critique du droit du travail* (Paris, Seuil, 1994).

[3] In most parts of the doctrine's idea, this intervention led to a labour law 'systematic de-structuration': Carinci, F, 'Introduzione – Dal Libro Bianco alla Legge delega' in F Carinci and M Miscione (eds), *Il diritto del lavoro dal 'Libro Bianco' al Disegno di legge delega 2002* (Milano, Ipsoa, 2002) 729.

of internal variations that may be described, in functional terms, as clusters of employment relationships formed in response to multiple interests. These aspects could be said to introduce a further flexibility within overall numerical flexibility.

For example, part-time work may now exist in 'mixed' forms that go beyond the traditional vertical and horizontal distributions. These include job-sharing (two or more individuals jointly entering into a single employment contract), job-splitting (subdivision of one full-time job into two part-time jobs), flexitime (where predetermined hours of work may be performed within variable limits on a daily basis, at the discretion of the employee) and the weekend contract.

Similarly, the fixed-term employment contract, even in those national systems that make use of them under general provisions (in Italy, for 'technical, organizational or replacement production reasons'), can be broken down into a series of categories in which numerical flexibility is achieved by collective autonomy (for example, of enterprises in a particular sector), quantitative limits on the establishment of new activities, provisions applying to specific disciplines (for example, air transport and airport services) or exemption from general rules (for example, tourism and public businesses, executives, companies engaged in export trade, import and wholesale of fruit and vegetables).

Agency work, in Italy called *somministrazione di lavoro* (article 2(1) of the Biagi law), is governed by fixed-term contracts or equivalent forms (for example, staff leasing) under which duties may be left unspecified or strictly defined. Work 'on call' (in Italy, *lavoro intermittente*: articles 33–40 of the Biagi law) is broken down into different types according to whether the worker is obliged to respond to the call or not.

The outcome of this process of contract diversification has produced a labour market that is both more complex, especially for groups suffering from high unemployment (youth and women), and highly segmented: a market in which large parts of the workforce remain at the margins of the production system, confined in precarious work with low levels of social protection and investment in training and poor chances of maintaining employment and career continuity. However, the situation no longer corresponds to the image of a labour market consisting of two large, separated and non-communicating aggregates (according to the traditional dualistic patterns: core/periphery, insiders/outsiders, primary/secondary, central/marginal, etc). The picture now seems much more nuanced, showing more points of intersection between the segments that compose it.

It has been debated throughout the first decade of the new millennium whether this pluralization of contract types, generally considered inevitable, should be controlled and rationalized (in an attempt to reduce, or at least to control, the proliferation of atypical patterns), or rather allowed free rein to disrupt the dominance of standard employment, following the rationality of the economic market.

The question we must now ask is a different one: how to conceive of a possible unitary recomposition of work.[4] For some time, we have witnessed a gradual shift

[4] The concept of 'unitary recomposition of work' can be found in many academic analyses in European law: see, eg, *cf* Supiot, A, *Au-delà de l'emploi* (Paris, Flammarion, 1999); Freedland, M, 'From the Contract of Employment to the Personal Work Nexus' (2006) 35(1) *Industrial Law Journal* 1.

from 'work' to 'works'; the road we should take now runs in the opposite direction, from 'works' to 'work' in general. The wide diversity of forms of work requires us, in fact, to rehabilitate the concept of 'work' in general and to rethink its protected status in broader terms.[5] We must begin to think of an alternative legislative strategy to replace that characterized by the plethora of different types of flexible contracts that for many countries has seemed to represent the only way to reform labour markets over the past two decades: one that allows for a better synthesis of the interests involved.

Academic analysts and the European Commission alike emphasize that any such unification of labour and protection under a new legal framework should not leave out the economically dependent self-employed.[6] Nor should consolidation necessarily lead to a reduction of protection; rather, the entire relationship between employment and protection in the labour market needs to be rethought. All business activities have an acute need for support, recognition and protection against risk, and these needs should be recognized in the general rules that govern labour mobility and competition.

We should therefore attempt to design a system of rules and paths that allows each worker to develop his or her personality and abilities through a progression of different roles and positions that correspond to legitimate aspirations, needs and capacities at different ages and in different circumstances.

Work, then, is envisaged in general as an area that is both rule-governed and characterized by mobility and freedom. This is the principle underlying, for example, the *contrat d'activité* proposed by Boissonnat in France in the mid-1990s. To conceive of a return to work in general in this way is not to abandon its personal, individual characteristics; this 'work' is not an abstract and impersonal construct, but a social activity performed by people in the same enterprise who build their common rules and share a sense of common endeavour.[7]

The key imperative is not solely to restrict the development of unstable jobs – because flexible work, whether welcome or not, is here to stay[8] – but to guard against its application to excess and implement all necessary measures to prevent workers from being 'imprisoned' without access to the guarantees provided under a traditional standard contract of work. A new security of labour needs to be constructed through new employment policies with the objective of building 'networks' to facilitate the transmission of benefits according to the 'flexicurity' paradigm.

[5] Supiot, ibid.

[6] See Perulli, A, *Economically Dependent/Quasi-subordinate (Parasubordinate) Employment: Legal, Social and Economic Aspects* (Brussels, European Commission, 2003).

[7] See Rullani, E, 'Lavoro immateriale e società della conoscenza' (2008) I *Paradigmi* 71 ff.

[8] See Gallino, L, *Il costo umano della flessibilità* (Roma-Bari, Laterza, 2001).

3.2 The Presuppositions of the Single Employment Contract

3.2.1 Protection and Employment: Questioning the Received Wisdom

It is against this background of the quest for a reunification of work that the concept of the single employment contract has emerged.

The idea of a single employment contract was proposed some 10 years ago by a few French economists, who suggested the creation of a 'système unique de protection de l'emploi'[9] and a 'contrat de travail unique'[10]. The objective was twofold: both to reduce the degree of segmentation that affects the labour market, and to reduce the rigidity of the standard employment contract, especially with regard to the matter of protection against layoffs for economic reasons, in order to create a more fluid labour market and thereby facilitate job creation by enterprises.[11] These French economists argued that the segmentation of the labour market is the result of strong protection granted to insiders (the holders of standard employment contracts), which prompts the increased use of atypical contracts: that is, insufficient flexibility in the standard contract leads to a search for greater flexibility by other means. The corollary of this analysis is that reducing the protection offered under the standard contract would make the labour market more dynamic and hence reduce segmentation. These theoretical assumptions underlie the debate over the relationship between the rigidity of the employment contract in respect of the protection it offers, labour market segmentation and the creation of new jobs (especially for young people).

Over the past two decades, the focus of debate on the relationship between the institutional framework of the labour market and economic development has shifted from inefficiency and bureaucratic rigidity (epitomized by the system of public employment) to the rigidity of the rules that govern not only the matching of supply and demand, but the administration of the employment relationship. Various assessments highlight the importance to the public interest of improving access to jobs by increasing adaptability and thereby restoring balance in the labour market.[12]

Since the issue of unemployment has been linked to wage rigidities, both real[13] and nominal,[14] the reform of industrial relations systems and labour legislation was seen

---

[9] See Blanchard, O and Tirole, J, *Protection de l'emploi et procédures de licenciement* (Paris, La documentation française, 2003).

[10] See Cahuc, P and Kramarz, F, *De la précarité à la mobilité: vers une sécurité sociale professionnelle* (Paris, La documentation française, 2004).

[11] Document d'orientation sur la modernisation du marché du travail et la sécurisation des parcours professionnels, du 18 juin 2007.

[12] See Nickell, S, 'Unemployment and Labour Market Rigidity: Europe versus North America' (1997) 11(3) *Journal of Economic Perspectives* 55 ff; Nickell, S, 'Unemployment: Questions and Some Answers' (1998) 108(3) *Economic Journal* 802 ff.

[13] See Phelps, ES, *Structural Slumps: The Model Equilibrium Theory of Unemployment, Interest, and Assets* (Cambridge, MA, Harvard University Press, 1994).

[14] See Gordon, RJ, *Macroeconomics* (Boston, MA, Addison-Wesley, 2003).

as the natural antidote to such rigidities. Theoretical support was drawn from the well-known 'insider–outsider' model,[15] endorsed by neo-Keynesian economists who sought the restoration of balance in the labour market through policies aimed at increasing labour mobility and wage flexibility, the redesign of unemployment compensation systems and modification of the rules on hiring and firing, in order to reduce costs. Studies by international organizations have increasingly indicated the rigidity of labour market regulation as a major source of unemployment and of the lack of ability to create new jobs in Europe.[16]

This trend in thinking has contributed to a widespread change in perceptions of the framework and functions of labour law over recent years. Labour law is increasingly seen as a means to create jobs, with a concomitant shift from the traditional concept of 'having' a job (with the emphasis on stability and uniformity) towards the 'being' of the person and on the individual's employability.[17]

From this perspective, which assumes a single, predominant way of facing the challenges generated by the contemporary phenomena on the macro level (economic globalization, technological innovation and demographic trends), the public interest provides a utilitarian justification of the flexibility needed to protect those in work and promote the creation of new jobs.

According to classical (and also Keynesian) economics, an inflexible labour market cannot function effectively as a mechanism for matching demand and supply of labour. The resulting mismatch will lead to persistently high unemployment, owing to legal obstacles to the mobility of production factors, and to wage levels that are not responsive to changes in the labour market.

However, notwithstanding this established theoretical argument, there is no empirical evidence that can confirm the effects of labour market deregulation on the rates of unemployment.[18] The flexibility of the labour market does not affect absolute levels of unemployment, having many different effects on flows and on turnover, and does not directly affect unemployment among particular groups of subjects (notably young people, long-term unemployed people and women).[19]

The OECD itself – which has for years identified flexibility as the main tool for achieving employment growth in most advanced industrial countries – has gradually revised its position, not only recognizing the empirical unsustainability of a clear correlation between flexibility and job creation, but also shifting the focus onto the negative effects generated by the indiscriminate use of flexibility, and indicating the need

---

[15] See Lindbeck, A and Snower, JD, *The Insider-Outsider Theory of Employment and Unemployment* (Cambridge, MA, MIT Press, 1988).

[16] See OCSE, *Croissance et inégalités. Distribution des revenus et pauvreté dans les pays de l'OCDE* (2008).

[17] See D'Antona, M, 'Il diritto al lavoro nella Costituzione e nell'ordinamento comunitario' *Diritto al lavoro e politiche per l'occupazione* (Atti del convegno di studio per il 50° anno della *Rivista giuridica del lavoro*, Napoli, 8 maggio 1999, 22 ff. (Meeting Proceedings for the 50th Anniversary of the *Labour Law Journal*, Naples, 8 May, 1999).

[18] See Esping-Andersen, G, 'Who is Harmed by Labour Market Regulations? Quantitative Evidence' in G Esping-Andersen and M Regini, *Why Deregulate Labour Markets?* (Oxford, Oxford University Press, 2000) 108, according to whom '"rigidities" have nothing directly to do with unemployment levels'.

[19] OECD, *Employment Outlook, 1999* (Paris, OECD, 1999), available at: http://www.oecd-ilibrary.org/employment/oecd-employment-outlook-1999_empl_outlook-1999-en

to find the right combination of flexibility, adequate levels of social protection and equity (in line with the guidelines promoted by the European Commission: see section 3.3 below).[20]

It must also be noted that the thesis outlined above has been challenged on a theoretical level by several studies arguing that there is no strict correlation between the 'protection' guaranteed by employment legislation and unemployment levels.[21] This theory is even contradicted by some of the OECD's own studies on the relationship between wage flexibility and employment: for example, the *Employment Outlook* for 1998 noted that neither economic theory nor econometric studies have been able to determine the influence on employment levels of legal or contractual stipulations on minimum wages.[22]

The same can be said for the relationship between growth in employment and restrictive legislation on layoffs: empirical studies have not been able to demonstrate that the law is excessively rigid, with negative effects;[23] on the contrary, it has been

[20] OECD, *Employment Outlook, 2004* (Paris, OECD, 2004), available at: http://www.oecd-ilibrary.org/employment/oecd-employment-outlook-2004_empl_outlook-2004-en

[21] See, eg, Nickell, 'Unemployment and Labour Market Rigidity', above (n 12) and Nickell, S and Layard, R, 'Labour Market Institutions and Economic Performance' (1998) Centre for Economic Performance, London School of Economics, CEP Discussion Paper No. 407, which contradict the hypothesis that the legislation on minimum wages and layoffs produces rigidities which have a negative impact on employment (which is linked, on the contrary, to other institutions regulating the labour market, such as the existence of overly generous unemployment benefits). More recently, similar considerations are expressed by Layard, Nickell and Jackman: Layard R, Nickell, S and Jackman, R, *Unemployment: Macroeconomic Performance and the Labour Market* 2nd edn (Oxford, Oxford University Press, 2005); and Del Punta, R, 'The Economic Challenge to Labour Law' in G Casale and A Perulli (eds), Compliance with Labour Legislation: Its Efficacy and Efficiency, Labour Administration and Inspection Programme (LAB/ADMIN) Working Document No. 6 (Geneva, ILO, 2010) 12. Consider also the analysis of Esping Andersen: Esping Andersen, G, 'Serve la deregolazione del mercato del lavoro? Occupazione e disoccupazione in America e in Europa' (1999) 56 *Stato e Mercato*; and 'Who is Harmed by Labour Market Regulations?', above (n 18), which emphasizes that there is no empirical evidence to confirm any effect of deregulation of the labour market on levels of unemployment. For a detailed reconstruction of opinions for and against the argument that labour flexibility offers a solution to employment problems, see the in-depth analysis of Deakin and Wilkinson: Deakin, S and Wilkinson, F, 'Il diritto del lavoro e la teoria economica: una rivisitazione' (1999) *Giornale di diritto del lavoro e di relazioni industriali* 587 ff; and Ashiagbor: Ashiagbor, D, *The European Employment Strategy: Labour Market Regulation and New Governance* (Oxford, Oxford University Press, 2005) 33 ff (to which reference is made for the many indications in the literature that there is no positive relationship between flexibility and employment).

[22] OECD, *Employment Outlook 1998* (Paris, OECD), 31, 42 ff, available at: http://www.oecd.org/employment/emp/oecdemploymentoutlook1998-towardsanemployment-centredsocialpolicy.htm according to which a reduction in minimum wage should facilitate youth employment and workers in professional training, but cannot be shown to have a general positive effect on all workers.

[23] In OECD, *Employment Outlook 1999* above (n 19) 47 and 68 ff, several studies demonstrate that rules on dismissal do not affect the overall level on unemployment, but rather affect its dynamic or its composition (eg, on turnover). This thesis is confirmed by other authors (Sestito: Sestito, P, 'La questione del lavoro e le interpretazioni proposte' in P Ciocca (ed), *Disoccupazione di fine secolo* (Torino, Boringhieri, 1997) 48 ff; Del Punta, R, 'L'economia e le ragioni del diritto del lavoro' (2001) 1 *Giornale di diritto del lavoro e di relazioni* industriali, 3, 19; and 'The Economic Challenge to Labour Law', above (n 21) 10 ff; Nickell, 'Unemployment and Labour Market Rigidity', above (n 12) 72; Esping Andersen, 'Serve la deregolazione del mercato del lavoro?', above (n 21) 67; Perulli, *Economically Dependent/Quasi-subordinate (Parasubordinate) Employment*, above (n 6) 357) and is reaffirmed in OECD, *Employment Outlook 2004* (above n 20) 63. See also: Ashiagbor, above (n 21) 43 (fn 59), which quotes some recent studies confirming the view that 'the EPL strictness has little or no effect on overall unemployment'; and Boeri and Garibaldi: Boeri, T and Garibaldi, P, 'Two tier Reforms of Employment Protection: A Honeymoon Effect?' Paper at: www.iza.org/conference_files/eplm2005/garibaldi_376 (2005) 2 (with other citations).

shown that a 'reasonable' protection against dismissal may have positive consequences.[24] The European Parliament itself, commenting on the Commission's Green Paper, pointed out that 'recent studies of the OECD and of other organizations have shown that there is no evidence that reducing dismissal protection and weakening of standard employment contracts facilitates employment growth', and that, on the contrary, there are European countries that demonstrate clearly 'that a high level of protection against dismissal . . . is fully compatible with high employment growth'.[25] It was also stressed that there is no proven correlation between loosening of constraints on dismissal and an increased propensity to take on employees; national studies, in fact, show the opposite, namely the persistence of high rates of employment in the presence of strong regulations on dismissals.

The above review of the arguments calls into question the main basis for economic criticism of labour law, according to which it detracts from the efficient functioning of the labour market. As we have seen, this analysis is not supported by empirical evidence – that is, the demonstration of a direct and unique cause–effect relationship between employment protection and unemployment rates – so it may be said that these theories are unable to demonstrate convincingly the irrationality of labour law from an economic point of view.[26]

On the contrary, as demonstrated by the experiences of several European countries (for example, the Netherlands and the Nordic countries), growth in employment and declining unemployment can coexist with strong protection for workers and generous welfare programmes.

3.2.2 Effective System, Effective Market: The Search for Compatibility between Law and Economics

More generally, a system of labour regulation is needed to build and maintain an efficient market: in the absence of an adequate legislative framework, the labour market is unable to create and sustain the long-term cooperative endeavour which is one of the main objectives of the employment relationship.

Such considerations are particularly critical in systems that, according to the OECD indicators, have maintained or even enhanced the rigour of their labour protection standards. As we shall see, this is the environment considered in the European

[24] OECD, *Employment Outlook 2004*, above (n 20) 63, notes that protective legislation on dismissals 'may foster long-term employment relationships, thus promoting workers' effort, co-operation and willingness to be trained, which is positive for aggregate employment and economic efficiency'. See, on this matter, Ashiagbor, above (n 21) 43.

[25] European Parliament (2007) 5.

[26] See Del Punta, R, 'L'economia e le ragioni del diritto del lavoro', above (n 23) 36; and more recently Del Punta, R, 'Economic Challenge to Labour Law' in A Lyon-Caen and A Perulli (eds), *Valutare il diritto del lavoro* (Cedam, Padova, 2010) 77 ff.

Commission's Green Paper on 'modernization' of labour law,[27] which proposed weakening of protection against dismissal as a recipe for enabling outsiders to gain access to a system of safeguards based on the idea of flexicurity. The concept of 'flexicurity', while perhaps not itself an adequate alternative to the injustice inherent in ultra-competitive capitalism, certainly requires agreement on how it is to be implemented, for it will damage some powerful interests and will require a real social compromise.[28]

The evaluation of the flexibility of the labour market in terms of efficacy is related to a criterion that falls outside the legal arena. In essence it entails evaluating the regulatory rationality of labour law, that is, whether it is compatible with the efficiency of the economic system.[29] It is here that the potential arises for a deeper consideration of the relationship between law and economics, hitherto characterized, in this era of globalization, by the tendency to criticize labour law in the name of economic freedom.

A first issue concerns the effects of labour law (and its rigid regulations) on the self-regulating mechanisms of the market, opening up new spaces of action for a modern labour policy aimed at providing more tools by which workers can protect themselves in the labour market, in terms of information, training, mobility and social security protection for periods spent not working, etc.[30]

The theme is summed up, on the one hand, in the formula of 'information asymmetries' in the employment relationship and in the labour market, and the concomitant focus on their necessary correction. This line of analysis identifies a new interface between economic efficiency and labour law; however, it seriously underestimates (more or less consciously) the historic but enduring problem arising from the asymmetry of power between the parties to the contract,[31] which is a different issue from that of asymmetric information.[32]

On the other hand, the idea of strengthening workers' bargaining power in the labour market suggests an important evolution of labour law, along a continuum which leads from the protection of the worker in the employment relationship to the protection of employability, considered as a result of guarantees provided by an

[27] Commission, 'Modernizzare il diritto del lavoro per rispondere alle sfide del XXI secolo' COM (2006) 708; For a critical analysis of the EU document, see Perulli, A, 'Il libro Verde della Commissione europea: un'occasione mancata?' (2007) 1 *Aran notizie* 21; Garafolo, MG, 'Post-moderno e diritto del lavoro' (2007) I *Rivista Giuridica del Lavoro* 135: Leonardi, S, 'Sul Libro Verde "Modernizzare il diritto del lavoro per rispondere alle sfide del XIX secolo"' (2007) I *Rivista Giuridica del Lavoro* 145.

[28] See, on this point, Kramarz, F and Lyon-Caen, A, 'Questions sur l'accord du 23 janvier sur la modernisation du marché du travail' (2008) *Revue de Droit du Travail* 146. 'Un moindre mal en guise d'idéal pour nos pays prospères par temps de résignation aux bienfaits du capitalisme, une alternative aux désordres et à l'injustice semées par le capitalisme hyperconcurrentiel? Encore faudrait-il s'accorder sur les voies de sa réalisation, qui heurterait nécessairement de puissants intérêts et supposerait un authentique compromis social'.

[29] For a critique of this idea of evaluation, see Affichard, J, Lyon-Caen, A and Vernac, S, 'De l'analyse économique à l'évaluation du droit du travail' (2009) 11 *Revue de Droit du Travail* 631 ff.

[30] Del Punta, 'Economic Challenge to Labour Law' in A Lyon-Caen and A Perulli (eds), *Valutare il diritto del lavoro* (Cedam, Padova, 2010) 77 ff.

[31] For an interesting review of this classic theme, see Lokiec, P, *Contrat et pouvoir. Essai sur les transformations du droit privé des rapports contractuels* (Paris, LGDJ, 2004).

[32] As quoted by R Pessi, *Persona e impresa nel diritto del lavoro Diritto e Libertà: Studi In Memoria Di Matteo Dell'olio* vol 2 (Torino, Giappichelli, 2008) 444.

advanced and articulated system of public employment services and an active labour market policy able to 'interact with the system governed by the economy and even able – within respect for constitutional principles – to govern it'.[33] Such a system will be necessary to achieve the Lisbon objectives and to realize the principle of free movement within the European Union labour market,[34] but is still very far from being implemented in many European countries. Particularly lacking is the capacity of the system to support workers through transitions from one form of work to another, including the education and training necessary to qualify or re-qualify according to the demands of their chosen professional paths.

A second issue concerns the negative effects – regarding both business organization and the economic efficiency of the system as a whole – of the law and of judicial control over individual dismissals, and the proposal to replace this with incentive systems based on a calculation of the estimated cost of breaching the contract: a kind of efficient breach of contract applied to labour law.[35] What is in question here is the anti-economic impact of regulation on layoffs, seen as justifying a radical revision of legislation, as well as the final abolition of the judicial review function, which is considered uncertain, economically unjustified and irrational.[36] The proposal is to replace it with a sort of 'automatic filter' capable of neutralizing the justified objective reason for dismissal or, better, redefining it in purely quantitative terms (according to the doctrine of the firing cost)[37] or eliminating all costs of dismissal (according to the doctrine of employment at will).

From this perspective, the law's effects are evaluated in terms of a pure logic of costs: on the one hand, optimization calculations are simpler because legal uncertainties are reduced (especially those arising from judges' decisions); on the other hand, litigation becomes a purely monetary operation in which negative externalities are internalized, restoring the optimal situation that would produce the effective functioning of the market.

The economic analysis of labour law has, therefore, a very significant meaning in positive law to the extent that it tends to favour a principle of labour market efficiency based on economic circulation. In this model, the protection of employees in monetary form (via taxes on layoffs, subsidies, etc) is much more effective than administrative or judicial control, and efficiency is achieved by allowing easy termination of employment, with monetary compensation calculated at levels judged to best enhance the mobility of workers, in the expectation of a better functioning labour market and lower unemployment.

According to Richard Posner, the best proof that employment protection systems are economically inefficient is the fact that in the United States employment at will is

[33] See Bortone, R, 'Le tutele e i servizi nel mercato' in A Perulli (ed), *Il futuro del lavoro* (Matelica, Halley editrice, 2007) 22.

[34] See Valdes Dal-Ré, F and Zufiaur Narvaiza, JM, *Hacia un mercato europeo de empleo*, Ministero de Trabajo y Suntos Sociales (Madrid, Centro de Publicationes, 2006).

[35] See Posner, RA, *Economic Analysis of Law* 7th edn (Austin, TX, Wolters Kluwer, 2007) 119 ff.

[36] See Blanchard and Tirole, above (n 9).

[37] See Ichino, P, *Il lavoro e il mercato* (Milano, Mondatori, 1996) 127.

the normal form of employment contract.[38] Posner argues that the economic analysis of law relating to dismissal shows the economic utopia to be a labour market without legal or judicial intervention. He recognizes, nevertheless, that there are in the United States some regulatory mechanisms with a jurisprudential origin, based on the 'common law tort of unjust termination', which reproduce the principle of just cause for firing a worker. Consequently, the decision on dismissals cannot be reduced to a simple evaluation in terms of economic costs and benefits, as the theory would suggest; on the contrary, according to the economic analysis of law, a higher cost of dismissal corresponds to a lower capacity/willingness to pay wages to workers.

These models of labour market regulation based on the idea that employment protection systems are inefficient are highly questionable. As noted above, the existence of an inverse relationship between the rate of employment protection and employment levels has not been proved by the economic sciences. The OECD itself, in its annual reports on the Employment Protection Legislation Index – in which the scientific approach is also doubtful[39] – admits that the only detectable effects relate to turnover, without any direct relationship between job security and unemployment rates.[40]

The zero-sum formula by which the protection afforded to 'insiders' would be reduced in order to provide full protection to 'outsiders' seems to be based on a fallacious argument that seeks to demolish the most important right of workers – that of the stability of their work, which is the cornerstone of many labour law systems (not just the 'Mediterranean' ones). Without stability, the regulation of the employment relationship would be on a slippery slope that would lead inevitably to dissolution in the common law of contracts, perhaps assisted by some fundamental constitutional guarantees.[41] Given that no statistical evidence is provided for the existence of correlations between legislative deregulation and levels of unemployment, economic criticisms can only be strongly based on ideology, representing an attempt to eliminate the balance between conflicting interests provided by labour law under the guise of a rational and 'scientific' approach, justifying any managerial choice involving dismissal for economic reasons – perhaps excepting only limits on dismissal for discriminatory or fraudulent reasons – thus putting into action a power of dismissal based on purely monetary logic.[42] Again, it should be stressed that labour law, far from confining itself to a purely quantitative evaluation of factors measurable in

[38] See Posner, above (n 35) 348.

[39] On errors made by the OECD relating to the Employment Protection Index, see, for Italy, Reyneri, E, 'Luoghi comuni e problemi reali del mercato del lavoro italiano' (2006) IV *Diritto Lavori Mercati* 2 ff; also more recently, with reference to other statistical reports, such as the World Bank's *Doing Business 2009*, see Lassandari, A, 'Re-evaluating Labour Law' in A Lyon-Caen and A Perulli (eds), *Valutare il diritto del lavoro* (Padova, Cedam, 2010) 93 ff.

[40] See OECD, *Perspectives de l'Emploi* (2004) 67 available at http://www.oecd.org/fr/els/emp/perspectives-delemploidelocde2004.htm.

[41] On the value of stability, with some references to constitutional principle, see Ballestrero, MV, 'Il valore e il costo della stabilità' in MV Ballestrero (ed), *La stabilità come valore e come problema* (Torino, Giappichelli, 2007) 8 ff.

[42] See Ichino, above (n 37) 126 ff. In his opinion, the judge should control only 'that the real reason for dismissal is not an illegal reason, as for example political, religious, trade union, racial, etc for which the dismissal has to be considered as invalid'. For a critical perspective in French theory, see Gaudu, F, 'Des illusions des juristes aux illusions scientistes' in A Jeammaud, *Le droit du travail confronté à l'économie* (Paris, Dalloz, 2005) 101 ff.

numerical and monetary terms, attributes qualities to goods, to persons and to actors' behaviours.[43] However, there is no doubt that the economic analysis of law is penetrating labour law regimes, in particular introducing change in the treatment of dismissal, either directly or indirectly.

The direct approach has recently been taken by the Spanish legislature (law no 35/2010), which introduced a new notion of 'good economic reason' that unifies the individual with the collective termination of employment, and allows dismissals in the event of 'expected' losses by the enterprise; this introduces a category of dismissal on the basis of estimated outcomes that courts will still have to consider reasonable. This reform simplifies the dismissal process and reduces the cost of the unemployment compensation to be paid in case of wrongful dismissal from 45 to 33 days' pay for each year worked. From this perspective, the 'work' as good or service is treated in terms of its 'competitiveness', as emphasized by the reduction of dismissal costs. Not only has the level of compensation for wrongful dismissal been lowered, but the amount of compensation to be paid by the enterprise has also been reduced, with contributions made from a guarantee fund (Fogasa, established and regulated by article 33.1 of the Workers' Statute) funded by the state.[44]

France and Italy, by contrast, have taken the indirect approach to changing redundancy rules, primarily through a reduction of the time allowed for judicial consideration. For example, concerned by the need for 'legal security', the French legislature (Article 75, Law No 2005-32) has drastically reduced both the time within which the *plan de sauvegarde de l'emploi* (to keep the employee in the job) can be challenged (from four weeks to 15 days after each meeting of the *comité d'entreprise*: Article L 1235-7, al 1, *Code du travail*), and the limitation period for appealing against a collective redundancy on economic grounds, now reduced to 12 months in derogation from the general law (Article L 1235-7, al 2, *Code du travail*). It is still under discussion whether this provision also covers the use of personal appeal on the basis of 'real and serious cause', [45] or whether that remains subject to the usual five-year term.[46]

The facilitation of dismissals within a shorter period of time is one of the most sensitive tools used by the law under the influence of right-wing economic analysis to exclude or limit judicial review of the reasons for dismissal, as shown by the Italian experience. This is the approach taken in Italy under the so-called 'Collegato lavoro' (Law No 183/2010), the main theme of which is control over judicial discretion:[47]

---

[43] See Sachs, T, 'La raison économique en droit du travail. Contribution à l'étude des rapports entre le droit et l'économie' (Thèse de doctorat en Droit privé et sciences criminelles, 2009 à Paris 10, dans le cadre de Ecole doctorale Sciences juridiques et politiques (Nanterre) sous la direction de Georges Borenfreund) 543.

[44] See Martin Puebla, E, 'Espagne: radiographie d'une réforme' (2011) *Revue du Droit du Travail* 521 ff; Del Rey Guanter, S, 'El despido por causas empresariales en la Ley 35/2010: los nuevos articulos 51 y 52 c) del ET' (2010) 21/22 *Relaciones Laborales* 117 ff. See also, 'Labour Market Reforms in Spain and its impact on recruitement and employment' *Fundación 1 de mayo* (Madrid, February 2012).

[45] See ministerial circular of 30 December 2005, as well as Limoges CA, June 16, 2008, Official Bulletin 7 May 2009, No 127, 29, note H Vray.

[46] Cass soc 15 June 2010, Bull Civ V, no. 134.

[47] See Mazzotta, O, 'Il "Collegato lavoro": introductory note' (2011) *Questione lavoro* 5 ff; Ferraro, G, 'Il controllo giudiziale sui poteri imprenditoriali' in M Cinelli and G Ferraro (eds), *Il contenzioso del lavoro nella Legge 4 novembre 2010, n 183 (Collegato lavoro)* (Torino, Giappichelli, 2011) 3 ff.

the legislation has introduced a double limitation period for forfeiture, adding to the time for extrajudicial appeal a further period of 270 days within which the appeal court must necessarily follow. This complex administrative mechanism, whose purpose is clearly dictated by an imperative of economic order, severely limits the right of action in court, forcing the worker, for reasons of caution, to proceed not with extrajudicial action, but with an action in court. This means, in all likelihood, a multiplication of court proceedings, in open contradiction of the underlying legal principle of minimizing recourse to the courts.

Alongside these mechanisms for reducing judicial control in matters of redundancy *ratione temporis* are others that propose a total exclusion of judicial control from employment matters, as noted by Cahuc and Kramarz in the context of their proposal for a single employment contract. From the same perspective, the Spanish '100 economists' manifesto' has presented an alternative proposal for the reactivation of the labour market based on the introduction of a single employment contract.

3.3 The European Commission Perspective

Fighting segmentation in the labour market is one of the founding drivers behind the European Union's principles of flexicurity, agreed in 2007:

> The way European citizens live and work is rapidly changing. Four main reasons can be highlighted [one of which is] the development of segmented labour markets in many countries where both relatively protected and unprotected workers coexist ('insiders' and 'outsiders').[48]

The 2010 'Employment guidelines' endorsed by heads of state and government confirm that 'Member States should integrate the flexicurity principles [. . .] into their labour market policies and apply them [. . .] with a view to [. . .] combating segmentation [. . .]'. This political exhortation is repeated in several contexts, including the Europe 2020 flagship initiatives 'Youth on the Move' and 'An Agenda for New Skills and Jobs'.

An integrated flexicurity strategy should involve the combination of four dimensions (contractual arrangements, lifelong learning, active labour market policies and a social protection system), all to be implemented on the basis of supportive social dialogue. In this context, the proposal for a single employment contract highlights a policy option for the first of these four components and in no way implies a strict focus on flexible contractual arrangements as the only policy instrument to address labour market segmentation. On the contrary, the concept of a single employment

[48] Council conclusions on the common principles of flexicurity (November 2007), Bruxelles, SOC 476, ECOFIN 483.

contract implies more sustained access to training and rights as an integral part of that contract, as we will see below.

It is interesting to note the position of the DG for Employment, Social Affairs and Inclusion on the single employment contract:[49]

> Recent academic work by a number of well-known European labour economists suggests the need to develop a comprehensive strategy, based largely on flexicurity principles, in order to tackle labour market segmentation by providing a kind of roadmap to exit dualism. It is important to stress that such a strategy should encompass several policy initiatives tailored to national circumstances (ie no 'one-size-fits-all' strategy). The set of measures proposed includes the adoption of a 'single permanent contract', replacing the existing legal asymmetry between permanent and fixed-term contracts. Such contract would be characterized by employment security increasing concurrently with job tenure (eg through the gradual rise in severance payments rights).

However, the Commission says that 'the 'single contract' alone is unlikely to solve the problem of labour market dualism, as the use (or abuse) of temporary contracts is not solely linked to legal aspects concerning employment contracts but is also affected by production patterns, social dialogue practices, enterprises' human resource policies, etc.'.[50]

For this reason, the Commission suggests other accompanying measures such as 'the introduction of a minimum wage; universal eligibility for unemployment insurance regardless of the type of contract; and limiting the application of temporary contracts to specific circumstances, such as genuine temporary tasks or highly paid work'.

---

[49] European Commission for Employment, Social Affairs and Inclusion, in the Employment in Europe 2010 Report, available at: ec.europa.eu/employment_social/eie/index_en.html.

[50] See the report, 'Job Security – Facing the Challenges of Economic Change', produced by the French Conseil de l'Emploi, des Revenus et de la Cohésion Sociale for a discussion, available at http://www.cerc.gouv.fr/rapports/rapport5/report5cerc.pdf.

An Outline of the Single Employment Contract

4

4.1 Basic Structure and Application

The single employment contract is an open-ended contract[1] which has no fixed time limit, but, in contrast with existing open-ended contracts, encompasses a sufficiently long entry phase, a gradual increase of protection rights, increasing with seniority and a stability phase. The entry phase encourages job creation, while the progressive increase in the employee's rights from entry onwards provides for increasing job security without necessarily adversely affecting the employer, as uncertainties regarding the match between employee and job are resolved in the stability phase.

The idea of a single employment contract is addressed mainly to those countries with segmented labour markets, in order to stimulate the creation of a flexible but also secure labour market and to combat segmentation through incentives to employers. The proposal echoes suggestions developed by various economists in Italy (Boeri and Garibaldi), France (Blanchard and Tirole; Cahuc and Kramarz) and Spain (the authors of the '100 economists' manifesto', including Bentolila and Dolado). Each suggestion underwent political debate and some versions have been converted into draft Bills.

Protection for workers under the contract can be provided in two ways, both of which should be taken into account and fine-tuned when tailoring the contract to national circumstances and institutions: monetary and legal.

[1] Typically, fixed-term contracts expire automatically at the end of the term, whereas current open-ended contracts have no finite time limit and the just clause for dismissal applies from the day after the end of the trial period (usually a few months).

4.2 Monetary Compensation

The single employment contract should include rules for monetary compensation upon dismissal in order to provide income protection for the worker. This compensation should take the form of a scheme of severance payment that increases in seniority: the higher the worker's seniority, the higher the payment he or she will receive by the enterprise in case of layoff.

The right to monetary compensation would exist from the day of signature of the contract until its termination. These rights would increase during an 'entry phase' until they reached a maximum, at which point they would enter a 'stability phase'. The idea is to ensure income protection for all workers and to prevent enterprises from having routine recourse to easy termination of employment.

The pace at which monetary compensation is accumulated would depend on the characteristics of each national system. Nonetheless, this path would be transparent to both employer and worker from the very beginning of the single employment contract.

The moment at which the entry phase would give way to the stability phase would also vary from case to case, but in all cases integration into the enterprise and the increase in rights would have to be gradual so that no discrete step is taken from the entry phase to the stability phase. Ensuring the absence of any such marked step would avoid giving the enterprise any incentive to terminate the employment of a worker just before he or she enters the stability phase.

4.3 Legal Norms

In addition to monetary compensation, some form of legal protection would be introduced in the single employment contract. 'Legal norms' include all the legal provisions that regulate the termination of a contract, such as notice period, notification procedure, maximum time for claim, possibility of reinstatement etc.

The level of employment protection legislation (EPL) embedded in the single employment contract may vary according to the specificities of national systems and political constraints. One possible scenario would be to reduce the legal protection inherent in the contract (keeping only the basic protection against discrimination and some specified period of notice) and providing the bulk of protection via the accumulation of monetary compensation. In this scenario, the role of other labour market institutions, such as access to unemployment benefits and active labour market policies, is of paramount importance to guarantee the worker the necessary level of protection and support in case of dismissal, and should be designed in a way consonant with genuine flexicurity arrangements.

Another scenario, appropriate to countries such as Italy where EPL is at a high level and where its reduction alongside investment in other forms of protection would be difficult, given fiscal constraints, the single employment contract could introduce some level of protection which would vary over the lifespan of the contract. As with most existing contracts, the single employment contract would have a reasonable probation period, followed by a phase where the contractual relationship is then confirmed. During the probation period, both sides can withdraw from the employment relationship without the possibility of recourse to a court, and during this period the level of legal protection for the worker is minimal. (This period should be defined in accordance with ILO Conventions.) Following the end of the probation period and the confirmation of the employment relationship by a new contract, the worker is protected with increasing rights in terms of both notice period and severance payment, but recourse to the courts in case of dismissal is still limited. Finally, in the stability phase, the level of legal protection is similar to that applicable to open-ended contracts.

In a third scenario, legal protection could be maintained at the level laid down in labour laws for open-ended contracts for the entirety of the period.

In any of these scenarios, the legislature should clearly define how contracts are to be ended, simplifying the termination of open-ended labour contracts and the costs of dismissal. In current practice, open-ended contracts are ended in court cases under rulings of labour law judges; dismissal based on any discriminatory reason (sex, race, religion etc) will always remain illegal in any kind of scenario.

4.4 Other rights

Along with monetary compensation and legal norms, the single employment contract would include the accumulation of other rights. For example, workers under a single employment contract would be entitled to unemployment benefits in the case of dismissal. Social security contributions associated with the contract would also ensure that all the time worked under a single employment contract would count towards the accumulation of pension rights. Monetary training accounts could also be gradually accumulated throughout the contract.

4.5 The Anticipated Benefits of the Single Employment Contract

Under the use of fixed-term contracts at present, neither the worker nor the enterprise has much incentive to invest in the job in such a way as to enhance productivity.

If these employment relationships were to be governed by single employment contracts, such incentives would come into being. For example, the worker might decide to move house closer to work to save commuting time and have more energy to devote to work, or to obtain a higher qualification which would require him or her to spend time and money on study. Making these investments adds value to the job performed. The employer, on the other hand, might decide that the worker is ready to proceed to more complicated tasks within the enterprise, again adding value to the job; this would cost time and money training the worker on the job, which would be worthwhile if the worker were more likely to remain with the enterprise. Protection under the single employment contract will take away some of the uncertainty inhibiting such investments and therefore encourage both sides to invest time and financial resources.

It is also worth noting that human capital accumulated on the job is in itself a strong deterrent to dismissal. By offering the prospect of more stable careers, the single employment contract could help increase youth employment and thereby family establishment and birth rates, and also improve the sustainability of the pension system by shortening unemployment spells and encouraging savings.

Workers will not be rendered more precarious in existing jobs by the introduction of the single employment contract, because it will apply only to new contracts, which under the current legislation are often simple temporary contracts, and because it sets out a clear path to stability. First estimations concerning the Spanish proposal show that the single employment contract would be greatly beneficial to temporary workers and also to the unemployed, because as job stability increased more jobseekers would be engaged as the dismissal costs during the entry phase would be lower. For the enterprise, this contract would not necessarily increase the average expected firing cost because the rate of job loss would be lower than under the current legislation. In particular, comparing the response to the crisis in France and Spain, almost one-half of the increase in the unemployment rate in Spain would have been avoided had the gap between the dismissal costs of workers with temporary and permanent contracts been lower, as it is in France.

Another advantage from the point of view of the enterprise is the reduction in the degree of uncertainty arising from the simplification of calculating dismissal costs. By increasing the transparency of these costs and diminishing the likelihood of having to go to court, this type of contract increases enterprises' ability to adjust labour inputs according to their business needs without the involvement of labour law judges, creating a sense of certainty which will have a positive influence on hiring. It will also limit the existing costs of court cases for both enterprises and workers.

Overall, the single employment contract is not likely to add rigidity to the labour market because it merely provides incentives for enterprises to react. The single employment contract would also encourage the creation of new enterprises and therefore of new employment opportunities.

5 Contrasting Views of the Single Employment Contract

5.1 Introducing the Single Employment Contract

The single open-ended contract does not need to replace the other kinds of contracts, as it would apply only to new contracts signed, not to those already in existence. This would gradually generate flexibility spread out over the entire labour market, not just concentrated in a small area of it. This would avoid entrenching dualism and indeed contribute towards reunifying segmented labour markets.

Once implementation is complete, the single employment contract will simply become the natural contract. However, the transition from current usage of both open-ended and temporary contracts into a labour market which uses the single employment contracts universally (or in the vast majority of cases) can be expected to take a long time. In this context, some incentives to employers and workers may be created to facilitate the transition.

From the employer's perspective, costs associated with the single employment contract should be lower compared with other forms of open-ended contracts, so that hiring workers under this contract is less expensive than under temporary contracts. In a transition period, this could be achieved by targeted differentiation of social security contributions. In the same vein and more permanently, the cost associated with temporary contracts should also increase, so that employers have fewer incentives to hire under these arrangements and are encouraged to turn instead to the single employment contract. For example, the Italian Bill foresees the establishment of minimum remuneration (at present there is no minimum wage in Italy) for all workers under all kinds of contracts. It also foresees an increase in unemployment benefit contributions paid under temporary contracts, which are now lower than those paid for permanent workers. Making the single employment contract more attractive to employers in these ways would deter them from using temporary contracts unless they were really needed. These incentives could also be made conditional on the willingness of enterprises to expand employment levels.

From the worker's perspective, direct hiring or signing-up subsidies could be targeted at workers as an incentive for them to enter into single employment contracts. This would address a possible loss for those workers who would otherwise sign a 'traditional' open-ended contract. Although the majority of new contracts signed in the EU are currently of a temporary nature, some open-ended contracts are still signed for new jobs. Making single employment contracts more attractive would provide an incentive for workers to switch their preference from a traditional open-ended contract to the single employment contract.

5.2 Criticisms of the Proposal and Some Responses

The European Commission's proposal for a single employment contract as a possible tool to tackle labour market segmentation[1] has prompted criticisms from some sectors of civil society, trade unions and employers' associations, for different, often opposite, reasons. This section summarizes some of the main criticisms, and suggests responses to them.

5.2.1 Increasing Flexibility Might Damage Workers Who Are Currently Protected

Some critics have argued that current workers with open-ended contracts will end up with less protection if dismissals, while costly for enterprises, become easier. These workers might lose job protection since the opportunity for workers to challenge, in the courts, an enterprise's decision to make layoffs will be reduced during the first three years of service (in Italy) or at any time (in France and Spain, and in Italy under Ichino's proposal). In addition, the severance payment due in case of dismissal might be lower than the amount workers would currently get in cases of unlawful dismissal (and in some situations lower even than the amount currently payable in cases of lawful dismissal).

In response, it can be reiterated that the single employment contract will not harm those who currently have permanent contracts, for it would apply only to new recruitment, not to existing working relationships. Furthermore, the single contract is not a precarious contract as it is open-ended, albeit with rising protection rights over time, and once the entry phase has expired, the level of protection of current permanent contracts is reached. Lastly, one should remember that in segmented labour markets

[1] See European Commission, *Employment in Europe* (Brussels, 2010).

temporary contracts are the prevailing mode of entry into the labour market, although they still represent a minority of all labour force contracts.

5.2.2 Enterprises Will Have Less Flexibility in Recruitment

Enterprises may lose the 'easy' flexibility they currently have in being able to use a varying pool of short-term or fixed-term contracts. Enterprises will indeed need to spread their required labour input flexibility over their full staff base. This will entail more complicated staff planning.

Where a high proportion of temporary contracts are used, job turnover is likely to be higher because it is cheaper to fire workers during the entry phase. The single employment contract should fundamentally change enterprises' recruitment policies, sharply reducing the incentives to hire on temporary contracts and so making sure that entry into the labour market occurs for the most part on an open-ended (albeit modified) basis. Once the single employment contract becomes the normal mode of recruitment, the risk of layoff within the entry period would be distributed across all newly hired workers and not overwhelmingly concentrated among temporary workers. Those workers who turn out to be unsuitable for the job within the probation period would eventually be dismissed. This provides a reasonable and much needed degree of flexibility for enterprises. Overall, job turnover will decrease.

5.2.3 The Consolidation Period is Too Long

It has been alleged that the single employment contract breaches the ILO Termination of Employment Convention, 1982 (No 158) since the consolidation period is too long. The French *contrat nouvelle embauche* [The New Employment Contract] was repealed as a result of court judgments that declared it in contravention of Convention No 158. In 2007, the ILO declared that the two-year period of consolidation was too long to be reasonable, and that no dismissals without justification were permissible (Rapport du comité chargé d'examiner la réclamation alléguant l'inexécution par la France des conventions (no 87) sur la liberté syndicale et la protection du droit syndical, 1948, (no 98) sur le droit d'organisation et de négociation collective, 1949, (no 111) concernant la discrimination (emploi et profession), 1958, et (no 158) sur le licenciement, 1982, présentée en vertu de l'article 24 de la Constitution de l'OIT par la Confédération Générale du Travail – Force Ouvrière) [Report of the committee set up to examine the representation alleging non-observance by France of the Freedom of Association and Protection of the Right to Organise Convention, 1948 (No 87), the Right to Organise and Collective Bargaining Convention, 1949 (No 98), the Discrimination (Employment and Occupation) Convention, 1958 (No 111), and the Termination of Employment

Convention, 1982 (No 158), made under article 24 of the ILO Constitution by the General Confederation of Labour – Force Ouvrière] .[2]

It is worth recalling here some of the key international principles enshrined in Convention No 158. It applies to all branches of economic activity and to all employed persons. However, a Member State may exclude some categories of employed persons from all or some of the provisions of the Convention. For example, it may exclude workers engaged under a contract of employment for a specified period of time or a specified task; or workers serving a period of probation or a qualifying period of employment, determined in advance and of reasonable duration; or workers engaged on a casual basis for a short period of time. In addition, the text provides that adequate safeguards shall be introduced in the national system against recourse to contracts of employment for a specified period of time aiming at avoiding the protection resulting from Convention No 158.

Articles 4 and 5 of the Convention stipulate that 'the employment of a worker shall not be terminated unless there is a valid reason for such termination connected with the capacity or conduct of the worker or based on the operational requirements of the enterprise (including establishment or service)' and that the following shall not be considered to be valid reasons:

a. union membership or participation in union activities outside working hours or, with the consent of the employer, within working hours;
b. seeking office as, or acting or having acted in the capacity of, a worker's representative;
c. the filing of a complaint or the participation in proceedings against an employer involving alleged violation of laws or regulations or recourse to competent administrative authorities;
d. race, colour, sex, marital status, family responsibilities, pregnancy, religion, political opinion, national extraction or social origin;
e. absence from work during maternity leave.

The procedure followed before or at the time of termination is of crucial importance in considering the application of Convention No 158. The employment of a worker shall not be terminated for reasons related to the worker's conduct or performance before he or she is provided with an opportunity to defend him or herself against the allegations made, unless the employer cannot reasonably be expected to provide this opportunity. In any event, a worker who considers that his or her employment has been unjustifiably terminated shall be entitled to appeal against the termination to an impartial body, such a court, labour tribunal, arbitration committee or arbitrator. In order for the worker not to have to bear alone the burden of proving that the termination was not justified, the methods of implementation in accordance with the national legislation shall provide for one or both of the following possibilities: (a) the burden of proving the existence of a valid reason for the termination shall rest on

[2] See: www.ilo.org/wcmsp5/groups/public/---ed_norm/--relconf/documents/meetingdocument/wcms_087583.pdf.

the employer; (b) the independent bodies dealing with termination of employment cases shall be empowered to reach a conclusion on the reasons for the termination having regard to the evidence provided by the parties and according to procedures provided for by national law and practice.

In accordance with Convention No 158, if the deputed bodies find that termination is unjustified, and if they are not empowered or do not find it practicable, in accordance with national law and practice, to declare the termination invalid and/or to order or propose reinstatement of the worker, they shall be empowered to order payment of adequate compensation or such other relief as may be deemed appropriate.

In any case, a worker whose employment is to be terminated shall be entitled to a reasonable period of notice or compensation in lieu thereof, unless he or she is guilty of serious misconduct, that is, misconduct of such a nature that it would be unreasonable to require the employer to continue his or her employment during the notice period.

In case of termination of employment, a worker shall be entitled, in accordance with national law and practice, to: (a) a severance allowance or other separation benefits, the amount of which shall be based, inter alia, on length of service and the level of wages, and paid directly by the employer or by a fund constituted by employers' contributions; or (b) benefits from unemployment insurance or assistance or other forms of social security, such as old-age or invalidity benefits, under the normal conditions to which such benefits are subject; or (c) a combination of such allowance and benefits.

However, the single employment contract discussed in this document is specified in general terms only. Any specific single employment contract a Member State may decide upon would need to be articulated so as not to breach international labour standards, which clearly distinguish between the trial period that should be of a reasonable duration and the entry phase during which a worker can be dismissed only upon the payment of a gradually increasing severance compensation and possibly also with just reason and a notice period. Dismissal based on discriminatory reasons will remain illegal both in the entry phase and the stability phase.

Selected Proposals for Introducing the Single Employment Contract 6

6.1 Italy: The Debate about Flexicurity

In Italy, the rethinking of the relationship between employment protection and the labour market has been the subject of lively debate over several decades. It forms part of the 'safety valves' reform framework within which various proposals have been made, including suggestions for a decisive shift towards protection,[1] as indicated by the proposed Law no 848 of 2002 on the reform of the labour market,[2] which introduced a distinction between the income support given to suspended workers at the point of dismissal (redundancy payment or *cassa integrazione guadagni*) and that given to those who have lost jobs (unemployment compensation).[3]

The process of this rethinking is a road strewn with reforms that have never been implemented. The White Paper on the labour market of autumn 2001, which gave rise to the draft Law no 848 (subsequently cancelled), heralded a profound reorganization of labour protection, from the review and overhaul of article 18 of the Workers' Statute (dealing with employment protection) to reforms of the labour market and labour inspection services.[4] In essence, the new design set out to extend the minimum level of protection provided by the safety net, increasing payments

---

[1] See Libro Bianco sul mercato del lavoro in Italia, *Proposte per una società attiva e per un lavoro di qualità*, (Ministero del lavoro e delle politiche sociali, Rome, October 2001). On this project, see Biagi, M, 'Competitività e risorse umane: modernizzare la regolazione dei rapporti di lavoro' (2001) I *Rivista Italiana di Diritto del Lavoro* 257 ff; Alleva, PG, Balletti, E, Carabelli, U, Di Stasi, A, Forlani, N, Liso, F and Paci, M, *Tutela del lavoro e riforma degli ammortizzatori sociali* (Torino, Giappichelli, 2002).

[2] On this topic, see Cinelli, M, 'Riforma del mercato del lavoro e welfare' (2006) *Rivista del Diritto e della Sicurezza Sociale* 17; Cinelli, M, '"Nuovi lavori" e tutele: quali spazi per la previdenza sociale?' (2005) 24(2) *Rivista Italiana di Diritto del Lavoro* 225; Pessi, R, 'Tutele previdenziali e tutele assicurative nello scenario dei nuovi modelli negoziali' (2006) *Rivista del Diritto e della Sicurezza Sociale* 39; Sigillò Massara, G, *Ammortizzatori sociali di fonte collettiva e fondi di solidarietà nella riforma del Welfare* (Padova, Cedam, 2008) 154 ff.

[3] See Di Stasi, A, 'Gli ammortizzatori sociali tra "il cielo delle idée" e le più recenti novità legislative. Una introduzione' (2011) *Rivista Giuridica del Lavoro e della Previdenza Sociale* 339 ff.

[4] For an analysis of the labour inspection system in Italy, see Fasani, M, 'Labour Inspection in Italy' (2011) Working Paper No 11, LAB/ADMIN (Geneva, ILO) .

(financed by contributions) to levels prevailing elsewhere in Europe, thereby shifting the focus away from a purely welfare-based system towards one focused on protected mobility and reintegration of workers into the labour market.[5] This ambitious reform, which claimed 'zero cost' funding, to be attained by eliminating waste and rationalizing the system of financing the safety net measures, was widely criticized and eventually abandoned because of the radical opposition mounted by the CGIL (the largest national trade union confederation).[6]

A few years later, in Law no. 247 of 2007, the legislature attempted to strengthen the safety net through a rationalization of the existing institutions, assigning to the Government responsibility for issuing decrees to reform the system by creating two instruments of income support. The first dealt with unemployment, and was aimed at harmonizing the institutions created to foster labour mobility and the administration of unemployment benefit through the creation of a unique form of protection, aimed at both providing the unemployed with income support and bringing them back into work. The second set out to provide income support to suspended workers in the form of a universal payment that would overcome the distinction between ordinary redundancy payments, that is, those paid under the current laws, and extraordinary redundancy payments, that is, those paid after the expiry of the current laws under exceptional government decrees (*cassa integrazione guadagni ordinaria o straordinaria*).[7]

The reform was accompanied by policies to strengthen active labour market measures designed to promote stable employment relationships,[8] increase employment rates for women and young people and reintegrate into the labour market those workers most in need of protection.[9] But the issue of flexicurity, as understood at EU level, entered the Italian labour policy debate only in the context of amendments to legislation, through the reform proposals of draft Law no. 1418 of 2009 (put forward by Senator Pietro Ichino and others),[10] an ambitious response to the segmented Italian labour market, described by Ichino as 'cittadella degli inclusi ed esercito degli eslcusi' – a fortress of insiders and an army of outsiders.[11]

---

[5] See Tiraboschi, M, 'Il sistema degli ammortizzatori sociali: spunti per un progetto di riforma' in M Tiraboschi (ed), *La riforma Biagi del mercato del lavoro* (Milano, Giuffrè, 2004) 1105 ff.

[6] See Lagala, C, *La previdenza sociale tra mutualità e solidarietà. Percorsi nel sistema pensionistico e degli ammortizzatori sociali* (Bari, Cacucci, 2001).

[7] See Liso, F, 'Brevi appunti sugli ammortizzatori sociali e sui servizi all'impiego nel protocollo del 23 luglio 2007' in A Perulli (ed), *Le riforme del lavoro. Dalla legge finanziaria 2007 al Protocollo sul Welfare* (Matelica, Halley editore, 2007) 110 ff; Sigillò Massara, above (n 2) 170; Gentile, G, 'La riforma degli ammortizzatori sociali' in M Cinelli and G Ferraro (eds), *Lavoro, competitività, welfare. Commentario alla legge 24 dicembre n. 247 e riforme correlate* (Torino, UTET, 2008) 488 ff.

[8] Perulli, A, 'Subordinate, Autonomous and Economically Dependent Work: A Comparative Analysis of Selected European Countries' in G Casale (ed), *The Employment Relationship: A Comparative Overview* (Oxford, Hart Publishing; Geneva, ILO, 2011) 137–87.

[9] See Rosano, M, 'Il riordino dei servizi per l'impiego' in M Cinelli and G Ferraro (eds), Lavoro, competitività, welfare. C*ommentario alla legge 24 dicembre n. 247 e riforme correlate* (Torino, UTET, 2008).

[10] DDL (25 March 2009).

[11] On the DDL in exam, see Gottardi, D, 'Osservazioni alla proposta di Pietro Ichino' (2009) III *Rivista Italiana di Diritto del Lavoro* 114 ff.

6.1.1 The Single Employment Contract: The Debate

As noted in the report accompanying the Ichino Bill, a modern country cannot remain passive in the face of current labour market trends, exacerbated by the global economic crisis. These trends give rise to both unfairness (with increasing numbers of precarious long-term jobs) and inefficiency (by discouraging investment in stabilizing precarious workers). As one of the Bill's reviewers commented:

> If the current law remains in force, over the next two or three years of great uncertainty, most of the hundreds of thousands of people who are losing their old jobs due to the crisis may find new jobs, but if they do, they will be the most unstable and least protected jobs.[12]

This is because, in times of economic crisis and great uncertainty about the future, companies are discouraged from offering new workers guarantees of stable employment.

The Ichino Bill, composed of seven articles, seems to follow the substance of the proposal already advanced in France by the economists Cahuc and Kramarz, and implemented by the French Government in a document that stressed the need to reduce the segmentation of the labour market through the creation of a single contract of employment, and thereby to change the dominance of open-ended contracts, frequently seen as a 'brake on recruitment'. The Italian Bill aims to balance the conflicting requirements of flexibility (for the employer) and safety (for the worker) through a combination of legal provisions and collective agreement (see article 2, co 1). The expressly declared purpose is 'to reconcile the greatest possible flexibility for production facilities . . . with the highest possible security and with equal opportunities for all workers', who are eligible for a permanent contract if there is a 'position of substantial dependence' (article 2, paragraph 1(a)).

This reform has four methodological principles:

1. The replacement of the old regime should take place gradually, according to the layering[13] method, or by the application of the new regime only to cases that come into existence at a certain moment.
2. Implementation of the new arrangements should take place through agreements between the individual parties concerned, with the law acting as a guide for specific solutions constructed and tried out by the enterprise and trade union involved.
3. The aim is to create a system that is not based on public resources, but is able without cost to the public purse to relocate outgoing workers and to attract new ones.
4. In recognition that public employment and training services cannot on their own respond adequately to the needs of the labour market, enterprises should be given incentives to apply efficient policies to attract and retain workers.

[12] See the relations to the DDL n 1481, also published in (2009) III *Rivista Italiana di Diritto del Lavoro* (Giuffrè Editore) 97.

[13] See Saint Paul, G, 'On the Political Economy of Labour Market Flexibility' in *NBER Macroeconomic Annual 1993* (Cambridge, MA, MIT Press, 1993).

The core of the reform is the introduction of the so-called collective agreement of transition to the new system of job protection provided by article 2, in which

> a group of enterprises and one or more trade unions . . . establish a bilateral body with a joint management, or a consortium between them, in order to ensure that newly hired workers, in case of loss of employment, would have both income support and intensive support in the labour market, following standards not lower than those indicated in Art 3.

This protection system, which would be applicable to all workers employed after a certain point, could also be applied to existing employment relationships in the enterprise, provided that it is endorsed either:

> (a) by a trade union or coalition of trade unions that, in the most recent election of union representatives extended to all the enterprise workers, within the last three years, has achieved a total of more than half of the votes received; [or]
>
> (b) by a trade union or by a coalition of trade unions which, although not satisfying the requirement in para a), has submitted the collective agreement to a prior referendum to all workers and has received more votes than the total half of the votes provided' (Article 2, paragraph 4).

Because of its special nature, in order to take effect the 'transition contract' must be published and then deposited with the CNEL (National Economic and Labour Council).

Article 3 of the Bill regulates the agreement on redeployment (*contratto di ricollocazione al lavoro*) between the bilateral body or consortium and the worker. This applies to workers who, having successfully completed at least one year of post-probation employment, are dismissed for justified objective reasons, or for disciplinary reasons declared illegal by the court. This contract involves the provision of compensatory payments for up to four years, amounting to 90 per cent of final salary for the first year, 80 per cent for the second, 70 per cent for the third and 60 per cent for the fourth (with reference, however, to a maximum annual salary of €40,000). This mechanism, inspired by the Danish system, means that even if the worker remains unemployed for the four years, the total compensation payable will be equal to three years' wages (90 per cent + 80 per cent + 70 per cent + 60 per cent = 300 per cent); but taking social security contributions into account, the total cost of dismissal to the employer of dismissal is limited to two years' wages.

The bilateral body or the consortium is then required to ensure that displaced workers receive intensive support in their search for new jobs, and in the provision of training and retraining, with the aim of finding job opportunities that actually exist and are appropriate to the workers' capacities. In parallel, workers have an obligation to make themselves available for requalification initiatives and for starting a new job on a timetable equal to that which applied before the dismissal. The work done in this phase is directed by the bilateral body/consortium and supervised by a tutor.

If the employee has passed the probationary period, but has not completed a year of subsequent service, the bilateral body or the consortium is obliged to offer only the latter part of the relocation contract, not the financial provisions set out in article 3, paragraph a).

The worker is free to withdraw from the redeployment contract without notice, while the bilateral body may terminate the contract if the individual ceases to be unemployed or refuses a job opportunity or professional training or retraining without justification.

Article 4 sets out the financing of the scheme. The bilateral body or consortium is funded by contributions from the enterprise or group of enterprises which have signed the founding contract, and any contributions that may be due from the European Social Fund and the respective region. Each enterprise must give a guarantee for their workers' credits with the bilateral body or the consortium, in case of closure.

With regard to business or production units (small enterprises) that do not fall within the scope of article 18 of the Workers' Statute, the Treasury imposed a contribution of 0.5 per cent of gross wages of workers subject to the new protection regime.

Along the lines of the North European employment protection model, the Bill proposes a new framework for the regulation of dismissal, within which a worker dismissed for economic or organizational reasons (article 7) is eligible for compensation at the cost of the enterprise. These proposals apply not only to the traditional employee (article 2094 of the Civil Code), but also to the provider of services who works on a continuous basis and receives more than two-thirds of his or her wages from the same enterprise. The only exclusion applies where

> the work [is] performed in a position of autonomy and . . . at least one of the two following requirements are met: a) the gross annual salary exceeds 40,000 Euro b) the person in question is registered at the Bar, or in another professional order which is incompatible with the status of employment (Article 5).

Under these proposals, the employee is assumed to be employed on a permanent contract, except where covered by the transition contract or other collective agreement applicable in the production unit, or in other specific cases.[14] On this point, the Ichino proposal follows the philosophy of the single employment contract advanced by Boeri and Garibaldi, following the French and Spanish examples.[15] As we have seen above, the single employment contract tries to avoid the typological fragmentation of contracts characteristic of the segmented labour markets in a number of European countries. The proposed 'single contract' (proposed decree Law no 2630/09 and decree Law no 2000/10), provides for an entry period of three years during which the only protection in the event of dismissal is in the form of monetary compensation. After the three years, the consolidation of the contract would guarantee stable and permanent employment, subject to the current labour legislation.

[14] Seasonal contracts, a contract signed to replace another employee whose employment is temporarily suspended for any reason, contracts for performance, eg, a theatre season, recruitment for fairs, markets and other trade events of a temporary nature, or for other requirements generally considered occasional or extraordinary, and engagements with a fixed-term contract of at least three years for scientific or educational activities cannot be classified as contracts of indefinite duration.

[15] See Boeri, T and Garibaldi, P, *Un nuovo contratto per tutti*, (Milano, Chiarelettere, 2008) and also 'Il testo unico del contratto unico', available at: www.lavoceinfo.it.

In the Ichino proposal, however, the prohibition on illegal non-disciplinary dismissal would be replaced by economic compensation. In other words, the Ichino scheme differs from that put forward by Boeri and Garibaldi in terms of the protection provided to workers. The adoption of a single employment contract does not automatically confer full protection in the labour market. Enterprises could, in fact, practise a systematic withdrawal from the single employment contract before the end of the three-year entry period, followed by renewal of the contract, so that a new period of free dismissal would apply. To avoid such a result, it would be necessary to provide a legal limit similar to that laid down for the fixed-term contract, whereby such a contract may not be renewed more than once. This does not preclude enterprises continuing to conclude new single employment contracts with different workers, thus leaving open this option to be used as required.

This model of the single employment contract, then, does not ensure the elimination of a segmented labour market or the end of precarious work. It is easily possible that a worker hired to work under the single employment contract may be dismissed before the end of the three-year entry period and subsequently have to enter into another single contract with a different employer, and so on after another period of under three years, thus perpetuating the worker's precarious status.

In this respect, it is not at all certain that the proposed single employment contract represents a better choice than the fixed-term contract, either from the enterprise's viewpoint or in terms of social inclusiveness.[16]

6.1.2 The Single Employment Contract and Article 18 of the Workers' Statute

As Carinci has noted, legislative attention has up to now been concentrated on distinguishing the different types of contract. From now on, it is also necessary to consider the new article no. 8 of decree Law no. 138/2011 (now Law no. 148/2011) – a measure that has not yet been thoroughly enforced and is not well understood[17] – which allows workplace bargaining at the local level to derogate from the national level. Moreover, as has also been noted, a similar result to that intended by the single employment contract could be achieved by reducing the duration of the trial period (to the six months' maximum foreseen by article 10 of Law no. 604/66) and stipulating the provision of full protection on termination of employment over a longer period of time than currently applies. The challenge of overcoming the segmentation of the labour market would then become merely a decision of business administration (involving the consolidation of the contract), which the enterprise would be encouraged to do because of its investment in human capital though education and

[16] See Tullini, P, 'Proposte di revisione della disciplina del lavoro flessibile' in G Ciocca (ed), *Le trasformazioni del mercato del lavoro* (Macerata, EUM, 2011) 35.

[17] See Carinci, F, '"Provaci ancora, Sam": ripartendo dall'art 18 dello Statuto'. ('"Play it again, Sam": Recent Draft Laws on Art 18 st lav', WP CSDLE 'Massimo D'Antona' IT–138/2012.

vocational training. In fact, if the enterprise decides not to waste the investment made in human capital, this alone would lead the labour market to self-regulate spontaneously, converging on the single employment contract, because of the greater opportunities it presents and the protection of mutual interests it embodies.

On the contrary, the Ichino Bill proposal differs from the perspective of the single employment contract set out by Boeri and Garibaldi in eliminating judicial review of dismissal by distinguishing between disciplinary and discriminatory dismissal (article 6), on the one hand, and dismissal for economic and organizational reasons (article 7), on the other. The application of article 18 of the Workers' Statute would be limited to unfair disciplinary dismissal, dismissal for discriminatory reasons, and dismissal on a whim. However, the real protection guaranteed is limited by the option given to the judge to order only reinstatement in the workplace with zero or reduced compensation for damages, or compensation alone without reinstatement. Small enterprises remain exempt from the requirement to reinstate dismissed workers.

Under Ichino's proposal, the new category of dismissal for economic and organizational reasons is based on the notion of objective justification, understood as the expected loss for the entrepreneur above a certain threshold, were the employment relationship to continue. This proposal states explicitly that the best way to protect the worker from illegitimate dismissal appears to be not judicial review of the reasons for the termination of employment, but rather the imposition of a monetary cost to the entrepreneur that is equal to the loss expected and considered appropriate not by the entrepreneur but *by policymakers*.[18]

At the time of the dismissal notice, as stated by the provisions of paragraph 2, the enterprise must pay as the first component of compensation an amount equal to one-twelfth of gross pay as received in the last year for every year of work done, less the salary corresponding to the notice period which is due to the worker. The second component of the compensation should be covered by unemployment insurance provided by the bilateral body or consortium. Thus, the exemption from judicial review for dismissal dictated by economic reasons is not equivalent to 'free dismissal': 'the entrepreneur's choices are subject to an automatic filter, consisting of the cost of redundancy – the "firing costs" – which is much more effective and less onerous for both parties, than what can be expected under the judicial procedure'.[19]

In addition, the report on the Bill, in the section entitled 'On the matter of the constitutionality and public legitimacy of the exemption of the economic justification for dismissal from judicial control', provides explanations and defences in response to any challenges on the grounds of constitutional legitimacy, including the

[18] In this sense, see Blanchard, O and Tirole, J, 'Contours of Employment Protection Reform, trad It, "Profili di riforma dei regimi di protezione del lavoro"' (2004) I *Rivista Italiana di Diritto del Lavoro* 161 ff. Art 5, para 5, arguing that 'le esigenze economiche od organizzative che motivano il licenziamento non sono soggette a sindacato giudiziale, salvo il controllo, quando il lavoratore ne faccia denuncia, circa la sussistenza di motivi discriminatori determinati, o motivi di mero capriccio, intendendosi per tali motivi futili totalmente estranei alle esigenze economiche, organizzative o produttive aziendali'. If, however, the dismissal has been imposed on an employee who has completed 20 years of service, the company, given the increased protection against the older worker, will have to provide the justified economic, technical and organizational reason for dismissal.

[19] See Ichino, P, *Inchiesta sul lavoro* (Milano, Mondadori, 2011) 124.

principle of the enterprise's absolute immunity from paying economic damages, which is very often overlooked by the courts – an oversight that could itself be considered unconstitutional.

In addition, the ILO Termination of Employment Convention, 1982 (No 158) provides for compensation to workers dismissed without justifiable reason; the Ichino proposal, in providing for compensation for all workers dismissed for economic organizational reasons, regardless of the legitimacy or not of the dismissal, offers a greater protection than that required by international standards.

The reform proposed by Ichino has generated criticism and objections from various quarters. Some criticize the single employment contract as embodying an irrational belief that the complex reality of modern ways of working and producing can be confined within a single bargaining scheme, compressing into a rigid framework the multifarious forms of fixed-term contract in a misconceived concept that substitutes the monetization of the employment relationship for freedom of dismissal.[20]

According to this perspective, the introduction of the single employment contract is unnecessary owing to the presence in the Italian system of the apprenticeship contract, which already represents a first stage in the labour market before the award of an open-ended contract. In principle, at the end of the apprenticeship period, there is a strong possibility of securing permanent employment because of the interest of the enterprise in keeping its trained and skilled workforce.

Another set of critics complain that insufficient consideration has been given to the context in which the reform is to be implemented. They argue that in conditions of deep economic crisis, the focus should instead be on immediate measures, and the strengthening of administrative resources, in order to avoid recourse to anti-crisis measures that require welfare interventions.[21]

Others still[22] take the view that the introduction of a single employment contract in Italy would have some systematic consequences which would be inconsistent with the present system of labour law. Carinci, for example, asserts that it would be 'unsustainable', pointing out that an open-ended contract which has no obligation of reintegration into the enterprise is more precarious than a fixed-term contract which is covered for the entire period by this obligation. Moreover, a part-time contract is not in itself either stable or unstable; it all depends on whether or not article 18 of the Workers' Statute is applicable.[23]

Another criticism of the proposed reform is that it does not take into account the different realities in various parts of the country and the variation of the labour market across different economic sectors and different geographical areas.

Above all, it is argued that the boundary between insiders and outsiders, understood as a stark division between two heterogeneous blocks, is not as clear as the

[20] See Tiraboschi, M, 'Contratto unico fuori dal tempo' *Sole 24 Ore* (12 April 2011).

[21] See Mariucci, L, 'Le politiche del lavoro di fronte alla crisi' (2009) III *Rivista Italiana di Diritto del Lavoro* 127 ff.

[22] See Carinci, above (n 17).

[23] Ibid.

model suggests, but on the contrary is very unstable and blurred.[24] In this environment, the solution to the challenges posed by the economy to the regulation of the labour market cannot be drawn from the neoliberal teachings of law and economics, on the assumption that removing guarantees to workers will increase the chances of the unemployed finding jobs.

Critics also point out that when the actual dynamics of the Italian labour market are taken into account, the proposed new mechanism would seem to be attractive only to the medium and large enterprises of the North, which would gain the advantage of being able to hire young workers without the constraints of real protection against unjustified dismissal.

Such criticisms, however, ignore the positive improvements embodied in the new single employment contract, for example, the promotion of the concept of 'economic dependence', the 'absorption' of most forms of atypical work currently used by enterprises and the consequent return to limits on the use of temporary contracts.

What is certain is that the culture still dominant among Italian labour lawyers – at least the strand of thought expressed in the critical comments on flexicurity – does not seem ready to accept solutions which modify the principle of the stability of the workplace (symbolized by article 18 of the Workers' Statute) in favour of new social, procedural and transactional rights. According to Carinci, the debate on article 18 has focused attention on the single employment contract. As he notes,

> the alternative of the single employment contract does not involve any permanent removal but only a temporary de-activation of the reintegration procedure, applied to enterprises for all new recruits who can count on a permanent contract. Moreover, such a contract does not concern the existing workers but only those who will enter the labour market, so its impact would not be immediate, but would be scattered over time, making it difficult to imagine a real change in a short period of time.[25]

It is worth considering, moreover, that other legislative proposals – in particular Bills no 263/09, on the *contratto unico d'inserimento formativo* (CUIF or single entry training contract), and no 2000/10, on the *contratto unico d'ingresso* or (CUI or single entry contract) – seek to put into practice the idea of the single employment contract by replacing the mechanism of judicial control over layoffs with an incentive mechanism (through severance costs). These two Bills, with similar objectives in respect of employment policy, provide for the introduction of a new contractual instrument with the potential to become the typical form of recruitment, absorbing the existing contractual forms and reconfiguring them within a single legal scheme. In fact, these proposals do not envisage the creation of a new legal type, but rather present a 'way or a path, easier to access, that can encompass the advantages of flexibility and accommodate an alternative universe of atypical work'.[26] The proposed CUIF envisages the

[24] See Mariucci, 'Le politiche del lavoro di fronte alla crisi', above (n 21). He takes Fiat as an example and points out that applying the dualistic setting, insider workers employed for an indefinite period would be identified, without taking into account the consequences that might occur if the company had to finance the *cassa integrazione guadagni* (redundancy fund).

[25] See Carinci, above (n 17) 48.

[26] See Tullini, above (n 16) 37.

elimination of many atypical contracts (article 2, paragraph 6, draft law no 2630/09), so that the single employment contract would serve as an alternative even to training contracts; the CUI, on the other hand, even if it is viewed as potentially the 'typical' form of recruitment, does not change the rules in place. The effect of *reductio ad unum* achieved through the CUI is more attractive for the enterprise, allowing 'enterprises [to] save money in investing in the workplace and to keep it in the enterprise'.[27] Both proposals show some elements of convergence with the underlying flexicurity philosophy; however, these are expressed with less consistency and less planning of the north European kind compared with the Ichino proposal, especially regarding the strengthening of security measures in the labour market.

The dual-phase[28] structure of the contractual scheme outlined in these proposals shows the logic of progressive stability, with an element of increasing protection against individual dismissals. In cases of dismissal for economic reasons, the guarantees of stability are reduced while the security measures in the labour market are stronger. In particular, compared with the forms of entry flexibility available today, the CUI provides the worker with stronger protection, in the form of redundancy payments related to the duration of the relationship, whereas the CUIF provides a stricter regime in respect of employment termination for justified reason (article 6) and refers to labour market protections as part of a future reform of social security benefits (article 10).

Even these proposals – more cautious than Ichino's – have attracted some criticisms. On the one hand, it has been argued that

> it is not certain that the single employment contract will be for the employer equivalent to a fixed term contract . . . and why or how the worker may prefer this contract compared with a fixed-term contract with a reasonable duration, which always could be converted into a permanent contract.[29]

On the other hand, some have argued that the single employment contract might be used to disguise 'the rigidity related to the stability of a real job', through a contractual scheme that, however, seems to be 'reserved only for large minorities within the economic system'.[30]

In this sense, Mariucci considers the adjective 'single', though tempting, not the most suitable because, in reality, the proposal represents an additional contract; hence he suggests it would be better defined as the 'prevalent' contract (that is, the dominant contract in the field alongside others).[31] He makes two critical observations: first, that while the American labour market, among the most liberalized in the world, has long been held up as a model, the United States has a higher rate of unemployment than Italy; second, that the latest version of Ichino's proposals, in which article 18 will not apply for new recruits but will remain in force for those already employed, would

[27] In relation to DDL 2000/10.

[28] Tullini, above (n 16).

[29] See Magnani, M, *Diritto dei contratti di lavoro* (Milano, Giuffrè, 2009) 171.

[30] See Ferraro, G, *Tipologie di lavoro flessibile* (Torino, Giappicheli, 2009) 23.

[31] See Mariucci, L, 'L'analisi' *L'Unità* (5 January 2012).

introduce a new and unacceptable dualism between those who have already entered the labour market and those who aspire to enter.

On the other side of the argument the Italian Prime Minister, Mario Monti,[32] criticizing the current labour market dualism, supports the idea of a single employment contract, asserting that it could guarantee a 'real universal discipline' for the new workers.

As this brief review makes clear, the critical views are divided between conservative and innovative perspectives. These are also the terms of the debate on flexicurity as a comprehensive project of labour market reform which requires a radical approach to changing the trade-off between input flexibility and output flexibility; between income protection and active labour market policies.

6.2 France: The *Contrat de Travail Unique* (CTU)

6.2.1 The Origin of the CTU

In France, the proposal for a single employment contract, a homogeneous contract of indeterminate duration for all workers, called *le contrat de travail unique* (CTU), is aimed at eliminating the distinction between fixed term contracts (*contrats à durée déterminée* or CDD) and open-ended contracts (*contrats à durée indéterminée* or CDI), in order to address the problems of precarious employment, the duality between insiders and outsiders, the lack of personal support for the unemployed, the difficulty in changing course to ensure a professional future and the general volatility of employment contracts.

This idea of a single employment contract has been proposed by two teams of internationally recognized economists, Blanchard and Tirole,[33] and Cahuc and Kramarz.[34] The debate on its possible introduction in the French legal system was launched in 2007 during the presidential election campaign of Nicolas Sarkozy,[35] who proposed the implementation of a single open-ended employment contract, with progressive rights, albeit with weaker protection against dismissal for economic reasons.[36]

[32] See the Prime Minister's speech, 'Communication by Monti to the Senate' (17 November 2011).

[33] See for details Blanchard, O and, Tirole, J, 'Contours of Employment Protection Reform' MIT Department of Economics Working Paper No. 03-35 available at: SSRN: ssrn.com/abstract=464282 (1 November 2003) or dx.doi.org/10.2139/ssrn.464282 (12 February 2012) and the Italian version: Blanchard, O and Tirole, J, 'Profili di riforma dei regimi di protezione del lavoro' (2004) 1 *Rivista Italiana di Diritto del Lavoro* 161.

[34] See for details Cahuc, P and Kramarz, F, *Rapport au ministre de l'Économie, des Finances et de l'Industrie et au ministre de l'Emploi, du Travail et de la Cohésion sociale*, 6 December 2004 (Paris, La Documentation française, 2005).

[35] See Projets – Actu soc n 99/2007 du 16 avril 2007.

[36] The idea was to protect: 'Moins les emplois et davantage les personnes, grâce à la création d'un contrat de travail unique, à durée indéterminée, à droits progressifs, plus souple en matière de licenciement économique'. From Nicolas Sarkozy's speech of 18 December 2006 in Charleville-Mézières.

This proposal drew renewed attention to two reports on social security and work published a few years earlier: one by Blanchard and Tirole, which was presented to the Conseil d'Analyse Économique in 2003,[37] and one by Cahuc and Kramarz, published in 2004.[38] Both aimed at reducing the duality of the French labour market; both proposed a new single employment contract in order to limit the inequity arising from the excessive use of fixed term contracts and from the increasing complexity of the employment contract.

In particular, Cahuc and Kramarz targeted the following:

- The very specific procedures regarding internal and external reintegration that applied to enterprises in cases of collective redundancies.
- The lack of effort on the part of employers and workers to reach agreement about collective redundancies.
- The delays associated with dismissal procedures.
- The increased use of fixed term contracts since the early 1990s.[39]

6.2.2 The Content of the CTU

The open-ended contract specifies the role, professional qualifications and remuneration of the employee. It may be ended as a result of wrongdoing by the employee, by mutual agreement, by the ending of the activity for which the employee has been hired, or by decision of the enterprise on economic grounds.

Two key provisions characterize the system. First, enterprises will be able to dismiss workers freely. The role of labour tribunals will be significantly reduced, with no right of appeal against the enterprise's decision, except in case of discriminatory dismissal. (In this sense the French reform is stronger than the one proposed in Italy, because this means that there will be no judicial control over dismissals.)

Second, enterprises will have to bear the cost of their dismissal decisions: they will have to pay both a solidarity contribution to the state, in order to finance the insurance unemployment system (as they already do), and also an indemnity to the worker when the layoff takes place. Both the contribution to the state and the severance payment will increase with seniority, whether in terms of time in post (Blanchard and Tirole) or in proportion to the total pay received by the worker during the period of service (Cahuc and Kramaz). In addition, the latter suggest increasing the indemnity by a 'precarity bonus' during the first 18 months of service, in order to deter the over-use of short-term contracts. Thus, an employer who terminates a contract within this period would be obliged to give the employee a severance payment equal to 10 per cent of total wages received by the employee during the length of the contract, and to help the employee

[37] See Blanchard, O and Tirole, J, *Protection de l'emploi et procédures de licenciement* (Paris, La Documentation française, 2003).

[38] See Cahuc and Kramarz, above (n 34).

[39] See Mihman, N, 'Le contrat unique: une bonne idée?' (2007) 2 *IUS Labor.*

find another job, for example by assisting in the preparation of a CV and passing on contacts. The employer is required to contribute to the state solidarity fund, which is used to finance unemployment benefits, an amount equal to 1.6 per cent of gross wages paid to each dismissed worker; enterprises may avoid paying this solidarity contribution by offering placement services to dismissed workers. However, employees who have been in post for less than 18 months do not qualify for this service.[40]

6.2.3 Predecessors of the CTU: The CNE and CPE

The CTU recalls two previous French experiments, both of which failed. Both the CNE (*contrat nouvelle embauche*) and the CPE (*contrat première embauche*) were thought of as open-ended contracts, and contained a prohibition (once an initial trial period had been completed) on firing a worker without a real and serious reason (*une cause réelle et sérieuse*). The CNE was introduced in France in 2005 and abrogated in 2008. It was applicable only to enterprises with fewer than 20 employees. The main characteristic of this contract was its flexibility during the two-year period of 'consolidation', within which employers were allowed to fire employees at will and at short notice, without the need to justify the dismissal.

The CNE was used as a model for the CPE, a contract that the French Government tried (unsuccessfully) to introduce in 2006. The CPE was available solely to employees under 26 years of age and was intended to encourage enterprises with more than 20 employees to hire 'workers at risk', namely long-term unemployed young people, belonging mostly to disadvantaged social groups. The CPE provided for a trial period of two years during which, as under the CNE, the employer could dismiss the employee without the need to provide any justification. After protests from students, trade unions and the general public, the proposal was withdrawn.

Both these contracts aimed at overcoming the resistance of enterprises to hiring workers on open-ended contracts, by offering the enterprise the opportunity to establish whether the worker was really suitable before binding itself to a permanent contract. The proposals, while attracting considerable interest abroad, were rejected in France. The CNE was called a 'stillborn contract'[41] and was condemned by various decisions of French labour courts. In October 2007 it was judged by the ILO to be contrary to the Termination of Employment Convention, 1982 (No 158), which France had ratified. Flament and Sachs described the CPE as 'an unforgettable example of a law enacted but officially instructed by the head of the state to remain unimplemented',[42] and the CNE as a 'victim of a veritable infanticide', in a sense that

[40] See Lamyline, FR, *L'ANDRH ranime le débat sur le contrat de travail unique*, Liaisons Sociales Quotidien – Liaisons Sociales, Bibliothèque: Bref sociale, Rubrique: études et rapports, 2011.

[41] See in this sense, Flament, L and Sachs, T, 'Simplifier the droit du travail?' (2010) 9 *Revue de Droit du Travail* 489 'des dispositifs législatifs (. . .) son mort-nès (. . .)'.

[42] 'Example inoubiable de loi promulguée que le chef de l'Etat appelle officialement à ne pas appliquer'. See Flament and Sachs, ibid.

as 'soon as it was brought to the baptismal font, preparations for its funeral were already under way'.[43]

6.2.4 The Debate

The CTU is today at the centre of a lively debate.

Antoine Lyon-Caen, in discussing the proposals, noted that

> it is not certain that the government and the social partners will reach agreement on the single employment contract and on the security of a professional career. While this project is rooted in the idea of rendering the labour market more fluid and promoting more uncertainty, so for the workers' organizations, security means a programme for reducing the precarious jobs.[44]

In June 2011, the Association nationale des directeurs de ressources humaines (ANDHR) re-ignited the debate with a call 'to fight against the excessive use of CDD and interim contracts with a view to simplifying the labour code'.[45] The association, presided over by Jean-Christophe Sciberras, the human resources director of the Rhodia group, proposed the introduction of 'un contrat de travail unique sans notion de durée ou de motif pour en finir avec la précarité'[46] – 'a single employment contract irrespective of duration with a view to ending the precarity' – with particular application to young people, within the framework of a programme of social dialogue and the development of youth employment. This proposal was submitted to the labour minister, Xavier Bertrand, who suggested studying the CTU proposal with a view to substituting it for the current CDD and CDI.[47]

Trade unions were opposed to the idea of a single employment contract because they saw it as threatening to introduce precariousness into the standard employment relationship. For example, the Force Ouvrière (FO) trade union considers the proposal a '*flexibilité à outrance*' – a 'flexibility too far'. The FO's general secretary, Jean-Claude Mailly, believed that work placements during the years of education were sufficient to give young people the confidence they need to enter the labour market, without changing the rules of the employment contract. The unions and the ILO Committee of Experts also judged this new single contract to be contrary to the ILO's Termination of Employment Convention, which requires a 'real and serious reason' to terminate the employment contract. According to the union federation. Confédération Française des Travailleurs Chrétiens (CFTC), the CTU is a 'false good idea': essentially a CDD with a non-defined end, which makes workers even weaker in an employment relationship by virtue of its provisions on dismissal procedures. The

[43] 'Victimes d'un véritable infanticide, tel le CNE: à peine était-il porté sur les fronts baptismaux que les préparatifs de son enterrement se faisaient déjà entendre'. See Flament and Sachs, above (n 41).

[44] Lyon-Caen, A, 'Unité, simplicité, dialogue' (2007) *Revue de Droit du Travail* 1.

[45] Landré, M, 'Contre la précarité, les DRH prônent un contrat de travail unique' *Le Figaro* (16 June 2011).

[46] ibid.

[47] Bartnik, M, 'Un contrat de travail unique difficile à mettre en oeuvre' *Le Figaro* (17 June 2011).

CFTC suggested that, in order to combat precariousness in professional transfers over the working lifetime, a workers' statute should be introduced.[48]

Employers, too, were critical of the proposal, arguing that they would lose the clear advantage of being able to choose among many different contracts, selecting those that would best address their particular need for flexibility.

Most legal commentary is also very critical of this proposal. Morvan, for example, criticizes the contract for making legal dismissal dependent only on a severance payment,[49] and believes that its only objective is to reduce the multiplicity of contract types; France's social problems, he argues, are the result not just of the nature of the employment contract, but of many other factors.[50] By way of alternative, he proposes a better use of CDI contracts. The legislature should make it easier to end an open-ended contract ('more firing, more hiring') and create an alternative dismissal procedure, offering greater protection to workers exposed to employers' decisions to dismiss, which, if necessary, should be subject to judicial control.

Lyon-Caen, defining the CTU as a 'seductive suggestion', reminds us that fixed-term contracts were introduced for serious reasons, which cannot be ignored. 'We need to recall that a fixed-term contract or a project contract was not introduced in order to avoid the rules on termination of employment, but rather in response to deep necessities'.[51]

Another commentator argues that the Cahuc–Kramarz report totally absolves enterprises from their responsibilities because it transfers the obligation to retrain and redeploy the worker to the public employment services.[52] Also, as with the CNE, there remains the matter of compatibility with Article 4 of ILO Convention No. 158, which obliges the employer to have a good reason to fire a worker. This doubt has been stressed also by the Conseil d'Orientation pour l'Emploi (COE), which rejected the idea of a single employment contract as early as 2006, not only because of its potential divergence from Convention No 158 but on the ground that it would have a series of perverse effects, namely: the old CDD would be replaced by a new form of short-term contract; there would be a sort of judiciarization of the termination of the employment relationship, with each employee hired for a particular reason able to protest against the reason for his dismissal; and the elimination of the enterprise's obligation to redeploy dismissed workers could lead to a preference for a quantitative rather than a qualitative approach to recruitment. For these reasons, according to the COE's opinion, a mechanism has to be provided to manage the transition from the current contracts to a new juridical system, with a view to keeping the rights already established. In the COE's view, the single employment contract should review all the

---

[48] See Freyssinet, J, 'Francia, l'accordo sulla modernizzazione del mercato del lavoro' *Eguaglianza e libertà, Rivista di critica sociale* (23 April 2008).

[49] 'Il suffit de payer pour congédier': Morvan, P, 'La chimère du contrat de travail unique, la fluidité et la créativite' (2006) 11 *Droit Social* 959, 960.

[50] Ibid.

[51] See Lyon-Caen, A, 'Unique' (2007) *Revue de Droit du Travail* 421.

[52] See in this sense Mattei, A, 'Le contrat de travail unique est-il souhaitable?' *Lamyline.fr, Semaine Sociale Lamy* (4 January 2012).

recent legislative evolution in favour of planned management of employment and competences. In addition, the COE suggests the creation of a bonus–malus system for enterprises, relating to numbers of dismissals and of temporary employment relationships: contributions would be calculated on the basis of the total wages received by the enterprise's workers, and could be regressive, with a view to giving employers an incentive to retain their workforce. According to Kramarz, the bonus–malus system is justified on economic grounds:

> When an enterprise lays a worker off, it does not take into account the costs for the community – unemployment benefits, social networks, etc. Such a cost is a 'negative outsourcing'. The introduction of a bonus–malus which is proportional, for example, to the worker's security, to be paid to the employment agency by the enterprise, would internalise the costs of the enterprise itself.[53]

This new form of financing could be balanced by a smaller contribution to unemployment support funds and lower labour costs.[54]

Not all the legal commentary is so sceptical. Lagarde and Jeammaud, for example, consider the CTU 'rather a good idea', starting from the reflection that 'legal doctrine, following Montesquieu and Portalis, does not have a sympathy for uniformity', and noting that the existing employment contract has to be adjusted in most cases. They consider the attractions of the CTU from different perspectives: political; moral (more equity between insider and outsider workers); social; and economic (many economists affirm that in order to combat unemployment it is necessary to concentrate on the labour market's fluidity, which is more useful than fighting dismissals).[55]

6.2.5 The Labour Market Situation

The situation of the labour market in France is similar to that in Italy. On average, across the OECD countries, 75.9 per cent of the young employed are in permanent jobs; in the original six members of the EEC this rate drops to 47.8 per cent, and the recent economic crisis has exacerbated this situation of precarious work and unemployment for young people[56] In France, as well as in other countries such as Italy and Spain, the proportion of workers in stable employment is low. Cahuc and Kramarz pointed out in their report that more than 70 per cent of employment contracts are for a fixed term, and more than 50 per cent of those are not converted, on expiry, into open-ended contracts.

---

[53] Kramarz, F and Lyon-Caen, A, 'Questions sur l'accord du 23 janvier sur la modernisation du marché du travail' (2008) *Revue de Droit du Travail* 146.

[54] See Lamyline, FR, *Un prérapport du COE rejette l'idée du contrat de travail unique*, Liaisons Sociales Quotidien – 2006, Liaisons Sociales, Bibliothèque: BREF SOCIAL, Rubrique: études et rapports.

[55] See Lagarde, X and Jeammaud, A, 'Que penser du "contrat de travail unique"?' (2007) *Revue de Droit du Travail* 8.

[56] See Bartnik, above (n 47).

The CTU offers a possible solution to this problem, as noted above. Yet it is not the only one, and it would be neither straightforward nor fast to apply. It is indeed of vital importance to evaluate the impact that a single employment contract would have on the whole system. This requires taking into account the current employment contracts, the transfer from an old contract to a new one, the renewal of the unemployment insurance system and the development of a real social dialogue with the trade unions to define the exact content of the contract, including the setting of limits on the employer's power of dismissal, which should continue to be subject to judicial control.

In truth, labour market dualism is one of the most serious problems of the French economy, but it is not the only one. The CTU does offer a possible path to follow, but it has to be accompanied by a wider reform, based on a fundamental reconsideration of the crucial role to be played by enterprises in sustainable development, which cannot wait for the next generation of workers.

As Cahuc and Kramarz have pointed out, in order to attain the goal of career security, the development of the employment contract and the regulation of dismissal must be based on two complementary principles: (a) the recognition of the social value of employment and protection of the individual; and (b) the implementation of the worker's right to upgrade his or her competences through training. The authors contrast the social value of employment with the value of employment to private enterprise. The former is the value of a job for the community, and its corollary is the impact of the loss of a job; the latter is the value of the production of goods and services by a worker, which is divided into pay for the worker and profit for the enterprise. The difference between the two values is measured by the loss of tax and social transfers consequent on the change in status of a worker from employed to unemployed or inactive.[57] It is therefore important to consider the social value of the job, including the tax represented by dismissal that imposes on the state an obligation to pay unemployment insurance, which is funded by the community.

Furthermore, the elimination of all the different types of contract would mean sweeping away all the developments in labour law of recent decades that have led to different employment contracts for different contexts (part-time, *contrat de mise à disposition*, *contrat de mission*, *travail temporaire*, *travail à temps partagé*, *contrat unique d'insertion*, *contrat d'apprentissage*, etc), in response to market demands for flexibility, and with a view to helping the weakest participants in the labour market. The need for this flexibility has not gone away.

This is probably the moment for an important reform in the French labour market, and if the debate about the CTU can offer an avenue towards a solution, it is worth continuing it.

---

[57] See Mihman, above (n 39).

6.3 Spain: The Debate on the Single Employment Contract

6.3.1 Introduction

In Spain, the topic of the single employment contract was introduced into academic debate on labour law in 2009 by the Fundación de Estudios de Economía Aplicada (FEDEA), a foundation supported by 100 economists, which proposed a single employment contract of indefinite duration for all new recruits, with a progressive cost of dismissal based on the seniority of the employee, ranging from eight days of annual salary up to a maximum of between 20 and 45 days of annual salary.

This type of contract would involve a radical change in two key elements of the labour relations model in Spain, namely the existing regimes on recruitment and on dismissal. In fact, such a measure would involve, first, the elimination of fixed-term contracts and second, simultaneously, the elimination of the existing system of dismissal, unifying hiring and firing discipline without distinction between individual and corporate layoffs or between fair and unfair dismissal. Thus, judicial review would be limited to dismissal involving violation of fundamental rights and disciplinary dismissal without compensation with a recognized possibility of appeal by the worker.

The debate on the single employment contract in Spain follows more or less the same trends as are apparent in other countries such as France and Italy. However, Spain is subject to particular pressure from high levels of unemployment. The most recent available survey data (EPA, January 2012) put the number of unemployed people at 5.27 million, representing a rate of 22.8 per cent of the workforce. This negative picture becomes even worse when the data are disaggregated to yield rates of youth unemployment, recognized as a cause of long-term exclusion from the labour market, and the number of families without either wage income or unemployment insurance. The ILO *Global Employment Trends 2012* report notes that 10 per cent of the total of 27 million jobs lost since the beginning of the economic crisis – 2.7 million new unemployed – were lost in Spain.[58] The report also reflects some other alarming rates, such as 48 per cent unemployment among people aged under 25 years in Spain, compared with 12 per cent across the rest of the world.

Nevertheless, grave though this picture is, the scale of unemployment rates, though certainly unacceptable for any country, cannot itself prescribe the outcome of legal debate about the suitability or non-suitability of a single employment contract. The solution a country adopts must fit its labour law system, with reference also to the constitutional framework, as well as to international and EU standards.

[58] See ILO, *Global Employment Trends 2012* (Geneva, ILO, 2012).

6.3.2 Factors in the Debate

The debate in Spain about the possible introduction into the legal system of a single employment contract is conducted on two levels: on the one hand, how it relates to the problems of the dual labour market, specifically those associated with temporary contracts and individual unfair dismissals; and on the other, the virtues attached to the single employment contract itself, as a solution to some of the structural problems that characterize the Spanish model of labour relations.

6.3.2.1 Fixed-Term Contracts and Unfair Individual Dismissals

Among the arguments against the introduction of the single employment contract, which would entail a cost of dismissal increasing with the worker's seniority, regardless of what their final role is, is a criticism based on the existing framework for hiring and dismissal.

In the Spanish model of labour relations, enterprises achieve the unilateral termination of employment in two main ways:

1. The use of temporary flexible contracts under articles 15.1 and 49.1.c of the Workers' Statute, primarily 'los contratos de obra y servicio determinado' (article 15.1.a), and 'los contratos eventuales por circunstancias de la producción' (article 15.1.b). These are contractual arrangements that allow easy termination of employment with a minimum charge of eight days' salary per year worked.
2. Recourse to the provisions for individual unfair dismissal under article 56.2 of the Workers' Statute, as amended by Law 45/2002 of 12 December 2002, 'de medidas urgentes para la reforma del sistema de protección por desempleo y mejora de la ocupabilidad'. These allow the enterprise to recognize the dismissal as unfair, and then to make available to the worker either 33 or 45 days' pay per year of service, depending on the type of permanent contract in question.

The problem concerning this dual system for the unilateral termination of an employment contract lies in the quantitative difference between the options available: in one case, eight days of salary per year of work, and in the other case, either 33 or 45 days per year of service, according to the type of contract.[59]

This regime incorporates another dysfunction, namely the facilitation of individual dismissals, thus avoiding both the impact of trade union bargaining power and judicial control over business decisions.[60]

The current dismissal model also generates a third problem, namely the recourse to redundancy for economic, organizational, technical and production-related reasons

[59] See Lahera Forteza, J, 'Elogio y crítica jurídica a la propuesta del contrato de trabajo único' (2010) 1 *Relaciones Laborales* 121.

[60] See Rodríguez-Piñero, M, 'Sobre el contrato de trabajo único' (2009) 10 *Relaciones Laborales* 8.

(covered by articles 52 (c) and 51 of the Workers' Statute), for which compensation is set at 20 days' salary per year employed. In practice, these are very marginal cases, compared with the massive use of temporary precarious contracts (*contrato de obra o servicio determinado*) under articles 15.1(a) and (b) of the Workers' Statute (the latter specifying their use in certain production circumstances).

Questions therefore arise on how best to apply a proposed single contract to the complex configuration of procedures for termination of employment relationships. For example, knowledge of what was required to prove the situation that justifies dismissal would ease the margins of uncertainty for the enterprise.

6.3.2.2 A Solution to Structural Labour Market Problems? Constitutional and Legal Perspectives

The key task at hand is to identify solutions that can be applied to the current situation. This is where the debate on the single employment contract arises, with arguments both in favour of and against it, in relation to its legal viability. The key arguments concern the constitutional perspective, especially articles 14, 24.1 and 35.1 of the Spanish Constitution; the possible violation of ILO Convention No. 158; and article 30 of the European Charter of Fundamental Rights.

With reference to the constitutional perspective, it has been noted that, first, there is a possible conflict between the single employment contract and the principle of equality under article 14 of the Spanish Constitution, as the new contract is reserved only 'for all new hires' ('para todas las nuevas contrataciones').[61] That would create an unconstitutional distinction between employees already in the labour market and future entrants after the introduction of the single employment contract.

Second, a possible violation of article 35.1 of the Spanish Constitution has been pointed out. This article expressly recognizes the labour law in stating:

> All Spanish people have the duty to work and the right to work, to free choice of profession or trade, to advancement through work and an income sufficient to meet their needs and those of their family, and to be free from discrimination on grounds of sex.

In particular, the Constitutional Court in its judgment no 20/1994 of 27 January 1994 stated that the substance of the right to work includes the right to job security, saying that 'the lack of proper protection against dismissal or removal dangerously weakens the consistency of the right to work' and that the law that regulates the protective function within the social sphere is an essential feature of the rule of law (referring to article 1 of the Spanish Constitution). Third, a possible violation of article 24.1 of the Spanish Constitution has been noted, considering that one of the main objectives of the single employment contract is to eliminate the judicial review of dismissals, except for dismissals based on discriminatory reasons, thus providing

[61] See Goerlich Peset, JM, 'Contrato único o reforma del despido por causas empresariales?' (2010) 1 *Relaciones Laborales* 78–79.

security and certainty for enterprises in their dismissal decisions, and enabling them to calculate in advance the costs of dismissal.[62]

Of all the objections outlined above, the most serious seems to be the difficulty regarding the principle of equality (article 14 of the Spanish Constitution). Even if the single employment contract were to substantially alter the mechanisms for ensuring stability in existing employment, it would still introduce differential treatment for new and established workers.[63]

The proposal for a single employment contract has also been submitted to review with reference to international and EU labour standards.

With respect to international labour standards, the adoption in law of this type of contract is at odds with the provisions of the ILO Convention on the Termination of Employment, 1982 (No 158). Regardless of the specific terms of its eventual formulation, unification of the dismissal regime to cover all reasons for dismissal, with the sole exception of those which are discriminatory or prejudicial to fundamental rights, is not consistent with the terms of the Convention, which states the need of a legitimate cause for termination of employment by the employer, and provides different legal effects for each cause of dismissal. As noted above, Convention No 158 distinguishes three levels of protection against termination of employment, and asserts that no employer can dismiss a worker in a capricious or manifestly arbitrary way.[64]

In relation to the legal obligations assumed under EU rules, Directive 98/59/EC on collective redundancies incorporates a distinction between the reasons that are inherent to the worker and those that are not (article 5.1(a) and (b)). This poses the main difficulty, in the case of collective redundancies, for the implementation of the single employment contract.[65] In short, the setting of a single level of compensation for dismissal under the single employment contract does not take account of the causes for dismissal and the different aspects covered by compensation and indemnity related to the termination of employment.[66]

For some critics, the single employment contract does not guarantee job security: it could even reduce it, increasing the turnover of employees, or enabling companies to use layoffs as a mechanism to proceed with the replacement of workers. Such effects would only exacerbate a more generalized job insecurity. A situation can be envisaged in which indefinite contracts subject to a legal regime of unfair dismissal would carry lower expected compensation than those currently in force.[67]

Notwithstanding the possible negative consequences of the introduction of a single employment contract, studies have also underlined some potential positive results of its implementation. One such would be its contribution to bringing together legal theory and actual practice in respect of recruitment at will and dismissal with legitimate

---

[62] Ibid, 79.

[63] Ibid, 80–84.

[64] Ibid, 86–87.

[65] Rodríguez-Piñero, M and Royo, MC, 'Algunos aspectos jurídicos de la propuesta de contrato único' (2010) 1 *Relaciones Laborales* 111–12.

[66] Rodríguez-Piñero, 'Sobre el contrato de trabajo único', above (n 60) 11.

[67] Ibid, 11–12.

reason. The single employment contract may be considered a factor contributing to the rationalization of dismissal costs and the generalization of the open-ended contract, as well as to a hypothetical revitalization of fundamental rights.[68] However, in the Spanish context, the single employment contract fails to address important risk factors. For example, there is a need to further explore how to deal with the difficulty of distinguishing between redundancy resulting from a worker's behaviour and dismissal for business reasons; how to integrate the procedures for collective redundancies with stronger worker participation in the enterprise; how to deal with the increase in litigation to be expected over dismissal for discriminatory reasons or in contravention of fundamental rights; the possibility of a new labour market segmentation between workers with open-ended employment contracts before and after the introduction of the single employment contract, and those future workers employed under this new contract; and finally, the risk of widespread job insecurity.[69]

6.3.3 A Lively Debate

As is clear from the discussion above, there is a lively debate in the legal literature on the possible introduction into the Spanish legal system of the single employment contract – a debate given particular edge by the country's high unemployment rates.

However, the problems of employment policies in a context of high unemployment cannot be allowed to obscure the rigorous legal analysis of the single employment contract vis-a-vis national constitutional principles (articles 14, 24.1 and 35.1 of the Spanish Constitution), the international framework (ILO Convention No 158) and European Union labour law (Directive 98/59/EC on collective redundancies).

All these elements raise serious questions about the suitability of the single employment contract for adoption into Spanish labour law, especially in respect of its provisions on hiring and firing. The majority of labour lawyers see undesirable effects ensuing in the form of a further dual model of fixed-term contracts and open-ended contracts, and the risk of a widespread use of unfair individual dismissals.

[68] Lahera Forteza, above (n 59) 125–27.
[69] Ibid, 127–36.

Contractual Arrangements in EU Labour Markets

7

In order to better understand the logic of the proposal discussed above, and to facilitate further analysis of the issues surrounding the introduction of the single employment contract, this section presents a brief comparative overview of the current contractual arrangements in the EU Member States.

Particular attention is paid to the following topics:

1. The protection for all workers against layoff at will, by forms of legal and/or monetary protection.
2. Clarity about this protection from day one of the contract.
3. Whether these protection rights build up continuously with job tenure.
4. Whether there are *ex ante* time limits to the contract.
5. Whether a sufficiently long entry phase is followed by a stability phase.

Typically, many contractual arrangements are available in national labour markets. However, the focus of the current discussion is on contracts that could be considered as 'mainstream' contracts, currently governing around 95 per cent of labour/employment relations. The following discussion does not take into account, for example, fluctuating seasonal work or independent highly skilled and specialized work undertaken by self-employed contractors.

In most labour markets, these mainstream contracts include 'open-ended' contracts (also known as 'permanent' contracts), 'temporary contracts'[1] and 'labour market insertion contracts'.[2] For these contracts, information on (a) the build-up of protection rights and (b) the cost structures in terms of social security contributions and tax treatment will shed light on labour market segmentation and the extent to which it may be caused by existing contractual arrangements. Furthermore, it will allow the Employment Committee of the EU to better organize the discussion on whether these contractual arrangements can deal with the pressing call for more labour market flexibility.

---

[1] Temporary contracts are contracts that are valid for a fixed period of time only.

[2] A labour market insertion contract is a temporary contract concluded with the specific aim of leading to an open-ended or permanent labour contract at its termination, if both parties so wish.

According to the available information, the most common form of employment contract in the EU-27 is the open-ended contract or the contract of indefinite duration. Where figures are available, the percentage of workers employed under such contracts varied quite considerably, from high levels in Lithuania (98 per cent) and Cyprus (87 per cent) to much lower levels in the Netherlands (66 per cent) and Portugal (61 per cent). Because these figures were taken from the total labour force including those workers defined as 'self-employed', they are lower than EUROSTAT figures which do not include these categories. Experts suggest that EUROSTAT figures (excluding the self-employed) are consistently higher. It is safe to conclude that all other reported percentages of workers employed under open-ended contracts would similarly fall if a more inclusive view were taken of what constitutes the labour force.

The most significant other form of employment contract reported was that for a fixed term or for a definite duration. Where specific figures were provided, the percentages of populations employed under such contracts ranged from 18 per cent (Portugal) to 4 per cent (Belgium). Other forms of employment contract reported include apprenticeship contracts (Austria, Ireland, Italy, Luxembourg); marginal employment contracts (Austria); freelance contracts (Austria); temporary agency work contracts (Austria, Estonia, Ireland, the Netherlands); project contracts (Italy); seasonal employment contracts (Greece, Hungary, Luxembourg); employment initiation contracts (Luxembourg); labour market insertion contracts (Portugal); and work performance/activity contracts (Slovakia). Some of these contracts – such as project contracts and work performance/activity contracts – clearly involve what elsewhere is described as 'self-employment' and consequently fall outside the scope of statutory employment rights and collective agreements.

7.1 Types of Protection Offered

A trial or probationary period is the period at the beginning of an employment contract – whether open-ended or fixed-term – during which (usually) both parties (but invariably the employer) have the opportunity to consider whether the job or the way it is being performed (depending on viewpoint) meets their expectations. If the contract is terminated during the trial period, the worker invariably enjoys less protection than if it were terminated thereafter. So, in Austria, for example, termination of the employment contract is possible during the trial period without any notice period and without giving any reason. In some cases (Belgium, Cyprus, Malta, Spain), the inclusion of a trial period in an employment contract is mandatory but its length can be determined by the parties to the contract. Only in the Czech Republic is there is a mandatory fixed trial period (three months). In most countries, the inclusion of a trial period in the contract is optional and its length is determined by parties to the contract. Table 7.1 provides an overview of the wide variation found in probationary periods across the EU.

Table 7.1 An Overview of Probationary Periods in EU Employment Contracts

Mandatory trial period		Optional trial period		
Fixed length	Variable length[a]	Short	Medium	Long
Czech Republic (3 months)	Belgium, Cyprus Malta, Spain	Austria, Belgium, Denmark[b] Netherlands[c]	Latvia, Lithuania, Poland, Portugal, Slovakia[d] Greece, Finland[e]	Bulgaria, Germany, Hungary, Italy, Luxembourg, Malta, Romania, Spain, Sweden[f] Cyprus[g]

[a] Decided by parties to contract.
[b] One month maximum.
[c] Two months maximum.
[d] Three months maximum.
[e] Four months maximum.
[f] Six months maximum.
[g] 24 months maximum.

The position in Ireland and the United Kingdom is different in that, although the parties to an employment contract are free to decide whether a trial period should be included, and if so of what length, protection against unfair dismissal applies only after a certain period of consecutive employment. At present, this is 12 months in both countries, increasing with effect from April 2012 in the UK to two years. In most countries it is found that, where applicable, trial periods apply equally to fixed-term contracts as to open-ended contracts.

The conclusion to be drawn must be that trial periods vary immensely across EU labour markets, between one and 24 months, but also within individual countries because in most countries the inclusion of trial periods is open as an option to contract parties.

A notice period is the period which either party must give in order to terminate an employment contract. The minimum notice period for open-ended contracts ranges from one week (Cyprus, Ireland, Malta, United Kingdom) to three months (Belgium, France – in both, with regard to 'white collar' workers only: see Figure 7.1). In a significant number of cases (Czech Republic, Denmark, Germany, Greece, Hungary, Latvia, Lithuania, Malta, Poland, Portugal, Romania, Spain, Sweden), it is reported that identical periods apply in the case of fixed-term contracts. However, in some cases (Austria, Belgium, Cyprus, Luxembourg) the relevant notice period is not applicable to fixed-term contracts.

In all EU Member States, employees in open-ended contracts are protected by unfair dismissal legislation; in some countries (Cyprus, Denmark, France, Germany, Ireland, United Kingdom) this applies only after a qualifying period of employment has been served. Only Cyprus exempts employees on fixed-term contracts from this protection; France and Netherlands reported that unilateral termination of such a contract was not possible. In Italy, the average length of unfair dismissal cases brought to labour courts and the uncertainty about their outcome (which, in larger enterprises, might lead to the re-employment of the dismissed worker) in many cases provide employers with an incentive to hire on a temporary basis.

Figure 7.1 Different Protection for 'Blue Collar' and 'White Collar' Workers

The type of protection offered to workers under open-ended contracts varies in some countries (Austria, Belgium, Denmark, France, Portugal, Romania) depending on whether the worker is regarded as being 'blue collar' (generally manual) or 'white collar' (generally non-manual). This distinction can have an impact, for instance, on the length of the trial period. In Belgium, for a blue collar worker the trial period varies between seven and 14 days, whereas for a white collar worker it varies between one and 12 months, depending on salary levels. In Austria, the length of the notice period depends on job tenure and ranges from six weeks to five months for white collar workers, while blue collar workers not serving under a collective labour agreement are protected by a notice period of two weeks only.

In a number of the countries mentioned above, labour market segmentation is reported between 'blue collar' and 'white collar' employees.

A statutory severance pay system for employees in open-ended contracts exists in almost all countries (with the exception of Finland, Romania and Sweden). Employees on fixed-term contracts are eligible for little or no severance pay in several countries (Belgium, Cyprus, Denmark, Finland, Italy, Lithuania, Luxembourg, the Netherlands, Portugal, Romania, Spain and Sweden). This is a clear difference in treatment which provides incentives to enterprises influencing their choice of contract type.

The nature and extent of statutory severance pay systems vary considerably. For nearly all countries (the only exceptions being the Czech Republic and Romania) job protection rights build up with job tenure. Generally this principle applies to the amount of severance pay (though not in Malta) and the length of the notice period (though not in Bulgaria, Finland, France, Italy, Latvia, Lithuania or Spain).

It is a relevant question whether this build-up of protection rights over job tenure is smooth or discontinuous. The way entitlements to severance pay builds up may influence enterprises' hiring/firing decisions and whether workers' contracts are continued and made permanent after the trial period has expired. In the Czech Republic, Poland, Portugal and Spain, it was indeed reported that such decisions are influenced by contractual protection rights.

On a more positive note, the assessment of some of the independent experts concludes that in other countries (Bulgaria, France, Germany, Hungary, Latvia, Malta, the Netherlands, Slovakia) the build-up of protection rights does not influence the hiring or firing decisions of enterprises or their choice of the type of contracts offered to workers. If and when these findings can be confirmed, for these countries contractual arrangements may be ruled out as a potential source of labour market segmentation.

Figure 7.2 Different Protection for Public Sector Employees

Some countries provide specific forms of protection for public sector employees through their contractual arrangements. For public sector workers in Slovakia and Spain, holiday entitlements for employees in open-ended contracts increase according to length of service. In Cyprus, employees in the private sector are paid less well and enjoy clearly lower levels of job security than public sector employees and those working for utility and natural monopoly enterprises (electricity, water and communication sectors).

Factors such as these may well cause segmentation between employment in the public sector and in the private sector.

7.2 Incentives to Convert Temporary Contracts into Open-Ended Contracts

In some countries (for example, Italy, Luxembourg and Spain), governments have introduced provisions creating incentives for enterprises to convert temporary/labour insertion contracts into open-ended contracts. Italy, for example, has seen various programmes aimed at encouraging enterprises to hire workers on permanent contracts. One such programme, in 2000, offered enterprises a subsidy of almost 5000 a year for each permanent employee hired. It was discontinued in 2006 because of lack of funding and allegedly considerable deadweight losses: it appeared that most of those enterprises claiming the subsidy would have hired permanent staff even without the incentive. In September 2011 the programme was reinstated, but with additional stipulations: the worker for whom the subsidy is paid must now be a parent aged under 35, and enterprises are eligible for the subsidy for a maximum of five new permanent hires. Incentives of this kind may well be needed given the low probabilities workers in these countries have of moving from a temporary contract to an open-ended contract.

7.3 Cost Structures and Financial Incentives in Choice of Contract Type

Generally, different cost structures do not provide financial incentives to workers and employers to prefer one type of contract over others. This is the case in Austria, Belgium, Bulgaria, Cyprus, the Czech Republic, Denmark, Estonia, Greece, Finland, Germany, Hungary, Ireland, Latvia, Lithuania, Luxembourg, Malta, the Netherlands,

Poland, Romania, Slovakia, Sweden and the United Kingdom. Denmark, however, draws attention to the use of 'one-man enterprises' especially in the construction sector. By hiring an individual as self-employed, the employer can avoid following employment protection provisions, social security provisions and collective agreements. This point may also be an issue in the Czech Republic, Germany, Estonia, Greece, Ireland, Hungary, Lithuania, Poland and Slovakia.

Only in Italy (explicitly) and Spain (implicitly) do different cost structures in terms of social security contributions represent an important financial incentive for employers to hire under fixed-term or temporary contractual arrangements, which carry lower costs.

Further Developments 8

Further comparative research and information gathering will be necessary before it is possible to present a well-founded opinion on whether or not it is necessary to introduce the single employment contract in a number of EU Member States. There remain significant questions to be addressed, chief among them:

- Is the single employment contract the solution to the problem of labour market segmentation?
- Are there other major features relating to contractual arrangements that need further analysis with a view to measuring their impact on segmentation?
- How can the contractual arrangements already available to the EU Member States contribute to reduce labour market segmentation?

These and many more questions need to be answered in order to reach a sound and well-grounded decision.

Conclusions

The analysis conducted so far has enabled us to reconstruct the features of the proposed single employment contract, placing it within the current scenario of the European labour market and its emerging problems. This is a context in which multiple vectors of change are interacting, giving rise to an urgent need for consolidation of law and practice. These changes include the growth of multiple flexible forms of contracts, especially at the beginning of the working life, increasing job insecurity and the prevalence of temporary work; and the increasing demand for greater flexibility in output and greater freedom in respect of dismissals, promoted with a view to boosting employment. In European countries that have adopted some form of the 'flexicurity' model, the search is under way for a new balance between flexibility and security.

The segmentation and casualization of labour that are typical of many European labour markets require a rationalization of flexibility instruments, which in some systems (Italy above all) appear to be out of control. From this perspective, the employment contract itself needs to be re-thought, and the introduction of a new provision that reduces the multiplicity of types of contract is most welcome.

The single employment contract is also supported by economic theory, introducing into employment arrangements the element of flexibility that is considered necessary in order to render labour markets more dynamic, creating new jobs, increasing turnover and hence presenting more entry points for 'outsiders'.

In addition, the single employment contract could be an opportunity to streamline legal systems in terms of workers' protection and the introduction of new guarantees inspired by the flexicurity model.

These are the potentially positive aspects of the proposed new contract. So far as the negative aspects are concerned, a series of questions has been raised, several concerning the technical–legal implications of its introduction.

From a business perspective, the single employment contract is an additional and unwelcome cost. Right from its original formulation by Cahuc and Kramarz, the model aims to recognize the social value (defined as the value for the community) of work by transferring to the enterprise the cost of the 'negative externality'/'negative outsourcing' represented by the termination of employment. Even in the form of a proposal advanced by Pietro Ichino in Italy, the social cost of dismissal rests with the enterprise. This is a major concern for business organizations. In France, the business community opposed the idea of the single employment contract for the same reason.

From the worker's perspective, it is claimed for the single employment contract that it would create a climate of security; but it is too early to say how effective it would be in this respect. The right to a stable job – guaranteed today in almost all European systems through judicial control of dismissal procedures – is modified in the single employment contract model through the introduction of the automatic filter of monetary compensation in case of dismissal and the concomitant reduction of the role of the judiciary in controlling procedures dealing with termination of employment. In essence, dismissal becomes a mere 'administrative practice' for the enterprise, calculated *ex ante* in terms of costs and benefits.

Moreover, in some countries there are still doubts about the compatibility of the single employment contract with the ILO Termination of Employment Convention, 1982 (No 158), with article 30 of the European Charter of Fundamental Rights, and with national constitutions, in respect of both unequal treatment (with different arrangements for new recruits and those already employed under existing contracts) and legal guarantees.

The pros and cons of the single employment contract will continue to be debated. What is really needed at this stage is a new balance between flexibility and security, but from a point of view of labour protection based on the employment relationship and not on the economic market alone. This would require the rethinking of social protection systems, creating the conditions for a more inclusive society in terms of income guarantees in the event of unemployment, along with a reconsideration of the nature of work, overcoming excessive fragmentation and insecurity. All these issues are unavoidable and common to all European legal systems.

There is a need for European and international institutions to take a more active role in addressing this task, and for a wider involvement of organizations representing the various interests involved, with a view to finding a broadly applicable and sustainable compromise to the current jobs crisis. The world of work needs it.

Annex

The Single Employment Contract Proposal

(Extracts from a note from the European Commission, EMCO/16/050411/EN, 2011)

The proposal for the single employment contract aims to reduce labour market segmentation as caused by the parallel availability of different contract types – which is currently the case in some EU labour markets. The idea of a single open-ended contract is a proposal relevant mainly to those countries with segmented labour markets. With this proposal the Commission does not prescribe one specific contract which will have to replace existing employment contracts. The Commission wants to bring forward a family of contracts, governed by an appropriate labour law, which share a number of characteristics set out below.

- The contract contains no ex-ante time limit.
- The contract specifies a sufficiently long 'entry phase', followed by a 'stability phase'.
- The labour law governing this contract generates a gradual increase of protection rights increasing with seniority.
- Protection is ensured along two lines which should be fine-tuned when tailoring the contract to national circumstances and institutions: monetary rights and legal rights.

Current legal practice does not include individual employment contracts which specify an increase of protection rights with seniority. However, it is practice in a number of labour markets that labour laws governing individual employment contracts – or the rulings of labour law judges in court cases – prescribe an increasing level of employment protection with seniority, with the protection coming from severance pay increasing with seniority.

The contract should include rules for monetary compensation upon dismissal in order to provide income protection for the worker. Protection should be defined in monetary terms following a structure of severance payment that increases with seniority: the higher the worker's seniority, the higher the payment he/she will receive by the enterprise in case of layoff. The presence of such a severance payment is intended to secure workers and to prevent enterprises from overusing their freedom to dismiss.

The right to monetary compensation would exist from the day of signature of the contract until its termination. These rights to severance pay, expressed in days per year of seniority, would increase during an 'entry phase' until they would reach a maximum after which the contract would enter a 'stability phase'. The increase of rights would have to be gradual so that no discrete step is taken from the entry phase to the stability phase to take away possible incentives which could lead to the enterprise firing the worker just before entering the stability phase.

The pace at which monetary rights are accumulated would depend on the characteristics of each proposal in respect of:

- initial severance pay level;
- rate of increase per year of seniority;
- length of entry phase;
- upper bound of severance pay.

The specific parameters of the single open-ended contract will need to reflect national labour market conditions and characteristics of the economy, and other available institutions providing protection to workers such as unemployment insurance, lifelong learning and ALMPs.

Besides monetary protection, some form of legal protection would be enshrined in the contract. Legal rights are all the legal provisions that regulate the termination of a contract such as notice period, notification procedure, maximum time for claim, possibility of reinstatement etc. Below, two scenarios are presented. These two are by no means exhaustive; the intention is only to show examples of what legal protection could be like in a single open-ended contract.

One first possible scenario would be to reduce consistently the legal protection inherent in the contract (basically keeping protection against discrimination and some notice period) and providing the bulk of protection via the accumulation of monetary rights. In such a scenario, the role of other labour market institutions such as access to unemployment benefits and active labour market policies is essential to guarantee to the worker the necessary level of protection in case of dismissal and should be designed in true integrated flexicurity arrangements.

In a second scenario, which could be suitable for countries experiencing high EPL and where, due to fiscal constraints, it would be difficult to couple a reduction of EPL with investment, the single open-ended contract could enshrine some level of protection which would increase during the lifespan of the contract. As with most existing contracts, the contract would have a reasonable probation period during which either side can withdraw without the possibility of recurrence to a court. In this period the level of legal protection for the worker is minimal. This period should be defined in accordance with ILO Conventions. After the probation period, but during the remainder of the entry phase, the worker is protected with increasing rights in terms of both notice period and severance payment but is still limited in their possibilities of going to court. Finally, in the stability phase the level of legal protection is that laid down in labour laws for open-ended contracts.

In any scenario, the legislator should clearly define how contracts are to be ended, increasing simplicity regarding the ending of open-ended employment contracts and the costs of dismissal. In current practice, open-ended contracts are ended in court cases under rulings of labour law judges. Dismissal based on discriminatory reasons (sex, race, religion etc) will always remain illegal in any kind of scenario.

Select Bibliography

Abraham, KG and Houseman, SN, 'Labor Adjustment under Different Institutional Structures: A Case Study of Germany and the United States' in F Buttler, W Franz, R Schettkat and D Soskice (eds), *Institutional Frameworks and Labor Market Performance: Comparative Views on the US and German Economies* (London, Routledge, 1995).

Affichard, J, Lyon-Caen, A and Vernac, S, 'De l'analyse économique à l'évaluation du droit du travail' (2009) 11 *Revue de Droit du Travail.*

Alleva, PG, Andreoni, A, Angiolini, V, Coccia, F and Naccari, G, 'La delega al Governo per il mercato del lavoro: un disegno autoritario nel metodo, eversivo nei contenuti' in PG Alleva et al, *Lavoro, ritorno al passato – Critica del Libro Bianco e della legge delega al Governo Berlusconi sul mercato del lavoro* (Roma, Ediesse, 2002).

Alleva, PG, Ballettim, E, Carabelli, U, Di Stasi, A, Forflani, N, Liso, F and Pacui, M, *Tutela del lavoro e riforma degli ammortizzatori sociali* (Torino, Giappichelli, 2002).

Altuzarra, A and Serrano, F, 'Firms' Innovation Activity and Numerical Flexibility' (2010) 63(2) *Industrial and Labor Relations Review.*

Arendt, H, *The Human Condition* (Chicago, University of Chicago Press, 1958).

Ashiagbor, D, *The European Employment Strategy: Labour Market Regulation and New Governance* (Oxford, Oxford University Press, 2005).

Atkinson, JG, 'Manpower Strategies for Flexible Organizations' (1984) 16(8) *Personnel Management.*

Auer, P, 'Security in Labour Markets: Combining Flexibility with Security for Decent Work' (2007) Economic and Labour Market Papers 12 (Geneva, ILO).

Ballestrero, MV (ed), *La stabilità come valore e come problema* (Torino, Giappichelli, 2007).

—— 'Il valore e il costo della stabilità' in MV Ballestrero (ed), *La stabilità come valore e come problema* (Torino, Giappichelli, 2007).

—— 'Il valore e il costo della stabilità' (2007) *Lavoro e Diritto.*

Barbera, M, 'Trasformazioni della figura del datore di lavoro e flessibilizzazione delle regole del diritto' (2010) 32 *Giornale di diritto del lavoro e di relazioni industriali.*

Barbieri, P, 'Lavoro flessibile e disuguaglianze in Europa' (2009) 25 *European Sociological Review.*

Barceló, C and Villanueva, E, 'The Response of Household Wealth to the Risk of Losing the Job: Evidence from Differences in Firing Costs' (2010) Banco de España, Working Paper No. 1002.

Bartnik, M, 'Un contrat de travail unique difficile à mettre en œuvre' *Le figaro* (17 June 2011).

Bentolila, S and Dolado, J, 'Labour Flexibility and Wages: Lessons from Spain' (1994) 18 *Economic Policy.*

Biagi, M, 'Competitività e risorse umane: modernizzare la regolazione dei rapporti di lavoro' (2001) I *Rivista Italiana di Diritto del Lavoro.*

Blanchard, O, *La disoccupazione in Europa: il ruolo degli shock e delle istituzioni* (Roma, Banca d'Italia Edizioni dell'Elefante, 1999).

Blanchard, O and Tirole, J, *Protection de l'emploi et procédures de licenciement* (Paris, La Documentation française, 2003).

——'Contours of Employment Protection Reform' (2004) I *Rivista Italiana di Diritto del Lavoro.*

——'Profili di riforma dei regimi di protezione del lavoro' (2004) 1 *Rivista Italiana di Diritto del Lavoro.*

Boeri, T and Galasso, V, 'Is Social Security Secure with NDC?' (2010) IZA Discussion Paper Series No. 5235.

Boeri, T and Garibaldi, P, *Un nuovo contratto per tutti* (Milano, Chiarelettere, 2008).

Bortone, R, 'Le tutele e i servizi nel mercato' in A Perulli (ed), *Il futuro del lavoro* (Matelica, Halley editrice, 2007).

Cahuc, P, 'Pour une meilleure protection de l'emploi' (2003) 63 COE–CCIP, Doc De travail.

Cahuc, P and Kramarz, F, *De la précarité à la mobilité: vers une sécurité sociale professionnelle* (Paris, La documentation française, 2004).

——'Le contrat de travail unique, clef de voute de la sécurité sociale professionnelle' in *Le droit du travail confronté à l'économie*, dir A Jeammaud (2005) *Dalloz.*

——*Rapport au ministre de l'Économie, des Finances et de l'Industrie et au ministre de l'Emploi, du Travail et de la Cohésion sociale* (Paris, La Documentation française, 2005).

Carinci, F, 'Introduzione – Dal Libro Bianco alla Legge delega' in F Carinci and M Miscione (eds), *Il diritto del lavoro dal 'Libro Bianco' al Disegno di legge delega 2002* (Milano, Ipsoa, 2002).

——'"Provaci ancora, Sam"': ripartendo dall'art 18 dello Statuto. ('"Play it again, Sam"': recent draft laws on art 18 st Lav', Working Paper CSDLE 'Massimo D'Antona'.IT–138/2012.

Caruso, B and Fuchs, M (eds), *Labour Law and Flexibility in Europe: The Cases of Germany and Italy* (Baden-Baden, Nomos; Milano, Giuffrè, 2004).

Casale, G (ed), *The Employment Relationship: A Comparative Overview* (Oxford, Hart Publishing; ILO, Geneva, 2011).

Castel, R, *La montée des incertitudes. Travail, Protection, Statut de l'individus* (Paris, Seuil, 2009).

Cinelli, M, '"Nuovi lavori" e tutele: quali spazi per la previdenza sociale?' (2005) 24(2) *Rivista Italiana di Diritto del Lavoro.*

——'Riforma del mercato del lavoro e welfare' (2006) *Rivista del Diritto e della Sicurezza Sociale.*

Cinelli, M and Ferraro, G (eds), *Il contenzioso del lavoro nella Legge 4 novembre 2010, n 183 (Collegato lavoro)* (Torino, Giappichelli, 2011).

——*Lavoro, competitività, welfare. Commentario alla legge 24 dicembre n. 247 e riforme correlate* (Torino, UTET, 2008).

Ciocca, G (ed), *Le trasformazioni del mercato del lavoro* (Macerata, EUM, 2011).

D'Antona, M (ed), *Politiche di flessibilità e mutamenti del diritto del lavoro: Italia e Spagna* (Napoli, Esi, 1990).

——'Il diritto al lavoro nella Costituzione e nell'ordinamento comunitario' Diritto al lavoro e politiche per l'occupazione (Atti del convegno di studio per il 50° anno della Rivista giuridica del lavoro, Napoli, 8 maggio 1999). (Proceedings of study for the 50th year of the *Labour Law Journal*, Naples, 8 May, 1999).

De Luca Tamajo, VR, 'Per una revisione delle categorie qualificatorie del diritto del lavoro: l'emersione del lavoro coordinato' (1997) 5 *Argomenti di Diritto del Lavoro.*

Deakin, S, 'Legal Diversity and Regulatory Competition: Which Model for Europe?' (2006) 12(4) *European Law Journal.*

Deakin, S and Wilkinson, F, 'Il diritto del lavoro e la teoria economica: una rivisitazione' (1999) *Giornale di diritto del lavoro e di relazioni industriali.*

Del Conte, M, 'L'influenza del diritto comunitario sul diritto del lavoro italiano fra tutele e flessibilità' in *Studi in Onore di Tiziano Treu* vol III (Napoli, Jovene editore, 2011).

Del Punta, R 'L'economia e le ragioni del diritto del lavoro' (2001) 1 *Giornale di diritto del lavoro e di relazioni industriali.*

——'The Economic Challenge to Labour Law' in G Casale and A Perulli (eds), *Compliance with Labour Legislation: Its Efficacy and Efficiency* (Geneva, ILO, 2010).

——'Economic Challenge to Labour Law' in A Lyon-Caen and A Perulli (eds), *Valutare il diritto del lavoro* (Padova, Cedam, 2010).

Del Rey Guanter, S, 'El despido por causas empresariales en la Ley 35/2010: los nuevos articulos 51 y 52 c) del ET' (2010) 21/22 *Relaciones Laborales.*

Di Stasi, A, 'Gli ammortizzatori sociali tra "il cielo delle idee" e le più recenti novità legislative. Una introduzione' (2011) *Rivista Giuridica del Lavoro e della Previdenza Sociale.*

Doeringer, P and Piore, M, *Internal Labour Markets and Manpower Analysis* (Lexington, Heath Books, 1971).

Esping Andersen, G, 'Serve la deregolazione del mercato del lavoro? Occupazione e disoccupazione in America e in Europa' (1999) 56 *Stato e Mercato.*

—— *Who is Harmed by Labour Market Regulations? Quantitative Evidence* in G Esping-Andersen and M Regini, *Why Deregulate Labour Markets?* (Oxford, Oxford University Press, 2000).

Esping-Andersen, G and Regini, M, *Why Deregulate Labour Markets?* (Oxford, Oxford University Press, 2000).

Eyraud, F and Vaughan-Whitehead, D, 'Employment and Working Conditions in the Enlarged EU: Innovations and New Risks' in F Eyraud and D Vaughan-Whitehead (eds), *The Evolving World of Work in the Enlarged EU. Progress and Vulnerability* (Geneva, ILO, 2007).

Fasani, M, 'Labour Inspection in Italy' (2011) Working Paper No. 11, LAB/ADMIN (Geneva, ILO).

Ferraro, G, *Tipologie di lavoro flessibile* (Giappichelli, Torino, 2009).

——'Il controllo giudiziale sui poteri imprenditoriali' in M Cinelli and G Ferraro (eds), Il contenzioso del lavoro nella Legge 4 novembre 2010, n 183 (Collegato lavoro) (Torino, Giappichelli, 2011).

Flament, L and Sachs, T, 'Simplifier le droit du travail?' (2010) 9 *Revue de Droit du Travail.*

Foucault, M, *Sécurité, Territoire, Population. Cours au Collège de France (1977–1978)* (Paris, Seuil/Gallimard, 2004).

Freedland, M, 'From the Contract of Employment to the Personal Work Nexus' (2006) 35(1) *Industrial Law Journal.*

——'Sur l'application du droit du travail et de l'emploi au-delà du contrat du travail' (2007) 146 *Revue International du Travail.*

Freyssinet, J, 'Francia, l'accordo sulla modernizzazione del mercato del lavoro' *Eguaglianza e libertà, Rivista di critica sociale* (23 April 2008).

Frouin, J-Y, Lamyline.fr, 'Discutant Droit du travail, droit du contrat et droit de l'emploi' Semaine Sociale Lamy – 1508 Supplément, 2011.

Gallino, L, *Il costo umano della flessibilità* (Roma-Bari, Laterza, 2001).

Garofalo, MG, 'Post-moderno e diritto del lavoro' (2007) I *Rivista Giuridica del Lavoro.*

Gaudu, F, 'Des illusions des juristes aux illusions scientistes' in A Jeammaud, *Le droit du travail confronté à l'économie* (Paris, Dalloz, 2005).

Gentile, G, 'La riforma degli ammortizzatori sociali' in M Cinelli and G Ferraro (eds), Lavoro, competitività, welfare. Commentario alla legge 24 dicembre n. 247 e riforme correlate (Torino, UTET, 2008).

Ghezzi, G, 'Dove va il diritto del lavoro? Afferrare Proteo' (2002) 3 *Lavoro e Diritto.*

Ghezzi, G and Romagnoli, U, *Il rapporto di lavoro* 3rd edn (Bologna, Zanichelli, 1995).
Goerlich Peset, JM, 'Contrato único o reforma del despido por causas empresariales?' (2010) 1 *Relaciones Laborales.*
Gordon, RJ, *Macroeconomics* (Boston, MA, Addison-Wesley, 2003).
Gottardi, D, 'Osservazioni alla proposta di Pietro Ichino' (2009) III *Rivista Italiana di Diritto del Lavoro.*
Grimshaw, D and Marchington, L, 'United Kingdom: Persistent Inequality and Vulnerability Traps' in F Eyraud and D Vaughan-Whitehead (eds), *The Evolving World of Work in the Enlarged EU. Progress and Vulnerability* (Geneva, ILO, 2007).
Guadalupe, M, 'The Hidden Costs of Fixed-term Contracts: The Impact on Work Accidents' (2003) 10 *Labour Economics.*
Guiomard, F, 'Le contrat nouvelles embauches à l'épreuve du contentieux prud'homal' (2007) 9 *Revue de Droit du Travail.*
——'Le contrat de travail' (2008) *Revue de Droit du Travail.*
Hamandia, A, 'Germany: Towards a Dual Labour Market?' in F Eyraud and D Vaughan-Whitehead (eds), *The Evolving World of Work in the Enlarged EU. Progress and Vulnerability* (Geneva, ILO, 2007).
Hohendanner, C and Bellman, L, 'Interne und externe Flexibilität' (2006) 5 *WSI Mitteilungen.*
Hunter, L, Mcgregor, A, MacInnes, J and Sproull, A, 'The "Flexible Firm": Strategy and Segmentation' (1993) 31(2) *British Journal of Industrial Relations.*
Ichino, P, *Il lavoro e il mercato* (Milano, Mondadori, 1996).
——*Inchiesta sul lavoro* (Milano, Mondadori, 2011).
ILO, *Global Employment Trends 2012* (Geneva, ILO, 2012).
Kongshøj Madsen, P, 'Reagire alla tempesta. La flexicurity danese e la crisi' (2011) 21(1) *Diritto delle Relazioni Industriali.*
Kramarz, F and Lyon-Caen, A, 'Questions sur l'accord du 23 janvier sur la modernisation du marché du travail' (2008) *Revue de Droit du Travail.*
Lagala, C, *La previdenza sociale tra mutualità e solidarietà. Percorsi nel sistema pensionistico e degli ammortizzatori sociali* (Bari, Cacucci, 2001).
Lagarde, X and Jeammaud, A, 'Que penser du "contrat de travail unique"?' (2007) *Revue de Droit du Travail.*
Lahera Forteza, J, 'Elogio y crítica jurídica a la propuesta del contrato de trabajo único' (2010) 1 *Relaciones Laborales.*
Lamyline FR, *Un prérapport du COE rejette l'idée du contrat de travail unique*, Liaisons Sociales Quotidien – Liaisons Sociales, Bibliothèque: Bref Social, Rubrique: études et rapports, 2006.
——*Le contrat de travail unique est-il souhaitable?* Semaine Sociale Lamy – 1297, Actualités, Débat, 2007.
——*Actualité sociale*, Liaisons Sociales Quotidien – Liaisons Sociales, Bibliothèque: Bref Social, Rubrique: Points de repère, 2011.
——*L'ANDRH ranime le débat sur le contrat de travail unique*, Liaisons Sociales Quotidien – Liaisons Sociales, Bibliothèque: Bref Social, Rubrique: études et rapports, 2011.
Landre, M, 'Contre la précarité, les DRH prônent un contrat de travail unique' *Le figaro* (16 June 2011).
Lassandari, A, 'Re-evaluating Labour Law' in A Lyon-Caen and A Perulli (eds), *Valutare il diritto del lavoro* (Padova, Cedam, 2010).
Layard, R, Nickell, S and Jackman, R, *Unemployment: Macroeconomic Performance and the Labour Market* 2nd edn (Oxford, Oxford University Press, 2005).
Leonardi, S, 'Sul Libro Verde "Modernizzare il diritto del lavoro per rispondere alle sfide del XIX secolo"' (2007) I *Rivista Giuridica del Lavoro.*

Lindbeck, A and Snower, JD, *The Insider-Outsider Theory of Employment and Unemployment* (Cambridge, MA, MIT Press, 1988).

Liso, F, 'Brevi appunti sugli ammortizzatori sociali e sui servizi all'impiego nel protocollo del 23 luglio 2007' in A Perulli (ed), *Le riforme del lavoro. Dalla legge finanziaria 2007 al Protocollo sul Welfare* (Matelica, Halley editore, 2007).

Lokiec, P, *Contrat et pouvoir. Essai sur les transformations du droit privé des rapports contractuels* (Paris, LGDJ, 2004).

Lundberg, J and Cronberg, E, 'Sweden: From Permanent to Temporary Employment Relationships' in F Eyraud and D Vaughan-Whitehead, *The Evolving World of Work in the Enlarged EU: Progress and Vulnerability* (Geneva, ILO, 2007).

Lyon-Caen, A, 'Unique' (2007) *Revue de Droit du Travail.*

——'Unité, simplicité, dialogue' (2007) *Revue de Droit du Travail.*

——'Un nouveau songe?' (2010) *Revue de Droit du Travail.*

Lyon-Caen, A and Perulli, A (eds), *Valutare il diritto del lavoro* (Padova, Cedam, 2010).

Magnani, M, *Diritto dei contratti di lavoro* (Milano, Giuffrè, 2009).

Mariucci, L, 'La forza di un pensiero debole. Una critica del Libro Bianco del lavoro' (2002) 1 *Lavoro e Diritto.*

——'Le politiche del lavoro di fronte alla crisi' (2009) III *Rivista Italiana di Diritto del Lavoro.*

——'L'analisi' *L'Unità* (5 January 2012).

Martin Puebla, E, 'Espagne: radiographie d'une réforme' (2011) *Revue de Droit du Travail.*

Matusik, SF and Hill, CWL, 'The Utilization of Contingent Work, Knowledge Creation, and Competitive Advantage' (1998) 23(4) *Academy of Management Review.*

Mazzotta, O, 'Il "Collegato lavoro" : introductory note' (2011) *Questione lavoro.*

Mihman, N, 'Le contrat unique: une bonne idée?' (2007) 2 *IUS Labor.*

Morvan, P, 'Le contrat de travail nouvelles embauches' *Juris-classeur Périodique* (Semaine Juridique) S, 2005, Etude, 117.

——'La chimère du contrat de travail unique, la fluidité et la créativité' (2006) 11 *Droit Social.*

——'Le contrat de travail première embauche' *Juris-classeur Périodique* (Semaine Juridique) S, 2006, Etude, 1289.

Moulier Boutang, Y, *Le capitalisme cognitif* (Amsterdam, Paris, Editions, 2007).

Muñoz De Bustillo Llorente, R, 'Spain: The Paradox of Job Insecurity Alongside High Employment Growth' in F Eyraud and D Vaughan-Whitehead, *The Evolving World of Work in the Enlarged EU: Progress and Vulnerability* (Geneva, ILO, 2007).

Nacsa, B and Köllo, J, 'Hungary: Employment Instability due to Fixed-Term Contracts' in F Eyraud and D Vaughan-Whitehead, *The Evolving World of Work in the Enlarged EU: Progress and Vulnerability* (Geneva, ILO, 2007).

Nickell, S, 'Unemployment and Labour Market Rigidity: Europe versus North America' (1997) 11(3) *Journal of Economic Perspectives.*

——'Unemployment: Questions and Some Answers' (1998) 108(3) *Economic Journal.*

Nickell, S and Layard, R, 'Labour Market Institutions and Economic Performance' (1998) Centre for Economic Performance, London School of Economics, CEP Discussion Paper No. 407.

Pedrazzoli, M, 'Dai lavori autonomi ai lavori subordinati' in G Giugni (ed) *Scritti in onore di Gino Giugni* (Bari, Cacucci, 1999).

Perulli, A, *Il potere direttivo dell'imprenditore* (Milano, Giuffrè, 1992).

——'Il diritto del lavoro fra crisi della subordinazione e rinascita del lavoro autonomo' (1997) 2 *Lavoro e Diritto.*

——'Lavoro coordinato' *Digesto, disc. priv. – sez. comm* (Torino, Agg. 2000).

Perulli, A, *Economically Dependent/Quasi-subordinate (Parasubordinate) Employment: Legal, Social and Economic Aspects* (Brussels, European Commission, 2003).

——'Lavoro autonomo e dipendenza economica, oggi' (2003) I *Rivista Giuridica del Lavoro.*

——'Il libro Verde della Commissione europea: un'occasione mancata?' (2007) 1 *Aran notizie.*

——(ed), *Le riforme del lavoro. Dalla legge finanziaria 2007 al Protocollo sul Welfare* (Matelica, Halley editore, 2007).

——'Per uno statuto del lavoro autonomo' (2010) 3 *Diritto delle Relazioni Industriali.*

——'Subordinate, Autonomous and Economically Dependent Work: A Comparative Analysis of Selected European Countries' in G Casale (ed), *The Employment Relationship: A Comparative Overview* (Oxford, Hart Publishing; Geneva, ILO, 2011).

——'Il diritto del lavoro tra libertà e sicurezza' (2012) 31(2) *Rivista Italiana di Diritto del Lavoro.*

Pessi, R, 'Tutele previdenziali e tutele assicurative nello scenario dei nuovi modelli negoziali' (2006) *Rivista del Diritto e della Sicurezza Sociale.*

——*Persona e impresa nel diritto del lavoro Diritto e Libertà: Studi In Memoria Di Matteo Dell'olio* vol 2 (Torino, Giappichelli, 2008).

Phelps, ES, *Structural Slumps: The Model Equilibrium Theory of Unemployment, Interest, and Assets* (Cambridge, MA, Harvard University Press, 1994).

Pinto, V and Voza, R, 'Il Governo Berlusconi e il diritto del lavoro: dal libro bianco al disegno di legge delega' (2002) I *Rivista Giuridica del Lavoro e della Previdenza Sociale.*

Posner, RA, *Economic Analysis of Law* 7th edn (Austin, TX, Wolters Kluwer, 2007).

Ray, J-E, 'La fausse bonne idée du contrat unique de travail' *Liaisons sociales magazine* (June 2006).

Reyneri, E, 'Luoghi comuni e problemi reali del mercato del lavoro italiano' (2006) IV *Diritto Lavori Mercati.*

Reynes, A, 'Variations sur le contrat de travail unique' D 2005, Chron 2348.

Revelli, M, *Oltre il novecento. La politica, le ideologie e le insidie del lavoro* (Torino, Einaudi, 2001).

Rigaux, M, *Droit du travail ou droit de la concurrence sociale?* (Bruxelles, Bruylant, 2011).

Rodríguez-Piñero, M, 'Sobre el contrato de trabajo único' (2009) 10 *Relaciones Laborales.*

Rodríguez-Piñero, M and Royo, MC, 'Algunos aspectos jurídicos de la propuesta de contrato único' (2010) 1 *Relaciones Laborales.*

Rosano, M, 'Il riordino dei servizi per l'impiego' in M Cinelli and G Ferraro (eds), Lavoro, competitività, welfare. Commentario alla legge 24 dicembre n. 247 e riforme correlate (Torino, UTET, 2008).

Roy-Loustaunau, C, 'Contrat de travail temporaire. Requalification de contrats successifs. Effet. Une seule indemnité de requalification et indemnités de rupture au titre d'un CDI unique' (2005) *Droit Social.*

Rullani, E, 'Lavoro immateriale e società della conoscenza' (2008) I *Paradigmi.*

Sachs, T, 'La raison économique en droit du travail. Contribution à l'étude des rapports entre le droit et l'économie' (Thèse de doctorat en Droit privé et sciences criminelles, 2009 à Paris 10, dans le cadre de Ecole doctorale Sciences juridiques et politiques (Nanterre) sous la direction de Gerorges Borenfreund).

Saint Paul, G, 'On the Political Economy of Labour Market Flexibility' in *NBER Macroeconomic Annual 1993* (Cambridge, MA, MIT Press, 1993).

Santoro-Passarelli, G, 'Competitività e flessibilità del rapporto di lavoro' (2009) I *Rivista Italiana di Diritto del Lavoro.*

Sennett, R, *L'uomo flessibile. Le conseguenze del nuovo capitalismo sulla vita personale* (Milano, Feltrinelli, 2001).

Sestito, P, 'La questione del lavoro e le interpretazioni proposte' in P Ciocca (ed), *Disoccupazione di fine secolo* (Torino, Boringhieri, 1997).

Sigillò Massara, G, *Ammortizzatori sociali di fonte collettiva e fondi di solidarietà nella riforma del Welfare* (Padova, Cedam, 2008).

Supiot, A, *Critique du droit du travail* (Paris, Seuil, 1994).

——*Au-delà de l'emploi* (Paris, Flammarion, 1999).

——*L'esprit de Philadelphie* (Paris, Seuil, 2009).

Tiraboschi, M, 'Il sistema degli ammortizzatori sociali: spunti per un progetto di riforma' in M Tiraboschi (ed), *La riforma Biagi del mercato del lavoro* (Milano, Giuffrè, 2004).

——'Contratto unico fuori dal tempo' *Sole 24 Ore* (12 April 2011).

Tullini, P, 'Proposte di revisione della disciplina del lavoro flessibile' in G Ciocca (ed), *Le trasformazioni del mercato del lavoro* (Macerata, EUM, 2011).

Valdes Dal-Ré, F and Zufiaur Narvaiza, JM, *Hacia un mercato europeo de empleo*, Ministero de Trabajo y Suntos Sociales (Madrid, Centro de Publicationes, 2006).

Wilkinson, F, *The Dynamics of Labour Market Segmentation* (London, Academic Press, 1981).

Index